12A

D1060107

GOD, FREE WILL, AND MORALITY

PHILOSOPHICAL STUDIES SERIES
IN PHILOSOPHY

Editors:

WILFRID SELLARS, *University of Pittsburgh*

KEITH LEHRER, *University of Arizona*

Board of Consulting Editors:

JONATHAN BENNETT, *Syracuse University*

ALLAN GIBBARD, *University of Michigan*

ROBERT STALNAKER, *Cornell University*

ROBERT G. TURNBULL, *Ohio State University*

VOLUME 27

ROBERT J. RICHMAN

Department of Philosophy, University of Washington, Seattle

GOD, FREE WILL, AND MORALITY

Prolegomena to a Theory of Practical Reasoning

D. REIDEL PUBLISHING COMPANY

A MEMBER OF THE KLUWER ACADEMIC PUBLISHERS GROUP

DORDRECHT / BOSTON / LANCASTER

FERNALD LIBRARY
COLBY-SAWYER COLLEGE
NEW LONDON, N.H. 03257

BJ
1012
·R484
1983

Library of Congress Cataloging in Publication Data

Richman, Robert J., 1923–
  God, free will, and morality.

    (Philosophical studies series in philosophy; v. 27)
    Includes index.
    1.   Ethics – Addresses, essays, lectures. 2.   Free will and
determinism – Addresses, essays, lectures. 3.   God – Addresses, essays,
lectures.   I. Title.   II.   Series.
BJ1012.R484   1983   123'.5   83–6786
ISBN 90–277–1548–3

Published by D. Reidel Publishing Company,
P.O. Box 17, 3300 AA Dordrecht, Holland.

Sold and distributed in the U.S.A. and Canada
by Kluwer Academic Publishers,
190 Old Derby Street, Hingham, MA 02043, U.S.A.

In all other countries, sold and distributed
by Kluwer Academic Publishers Group,
P.O. Box 322, 3300 AH Dordrecht, Holland.

93722

All Rights Reserved
© 1983 by D. Reidel Publishing Company, Dordrecht, Holland
and copyright holders as specified in the preface
No part of the material protected by this copyright notice may be reproduced or
utilized in any form or by any means, electronic or mechanical,
including photocopying, recording or by any information storage and
retrieval system, without written permission from the copyright owner.

Printed in The Netherlands

For Carol

TABLE OF CONTENTS

PREFACE

"He [Francis Bacon] writes of science like a Lord Chancellor"

— William Harvey

"Don't say: 'There must be something common ... ' — but look and see"

Ludwig Wittgenstein

In the history of western moral philosophy since Plato, there has been a pervasive tendency for the moral theorist to write, in effect, like a scientist, i.e. to seek completely general principles of right conduct. Of late, moreover, there has been an attempt to set forth a theory underlying the general principles, not of right conduct, admittedly, but of justice. To be sure, we are sometimes warned that the principles (which *must* exist?) may be too complex to be formulated. Also they may not exist prior to action — nonetheless, we are told, they serve as guides to conduct!

One might argue that Baconian inductivism provides one basis for skepticism with respect to a number of familiar epistemological problems. Thus, the skeptic argues, a certain conclusion — say, the existence of another's pain — is not justified on the basis of (behavioral) evidence either deductively or inductively, and hence it is not justified at all. Similarly, I should claim, by establishing an unattainable standard, the search for exceptionless principles may become a source of moral skepticism. After all, when confronted with a supposed principle designed to justify a particular

ix

action, one can generally imagine a counter-example to the principle without excessive difficulty.

In any event, the (modified) 'intuitionism' implicit in this rejection of general moral principles informs the essay which follows. Its bearing on the practical problem of freedom of the will will, I trust, become clear as the discussion proceeds. Roughly, the idea is that the persistence of this problem results from the acceptance of a principle — that 'ought' implies 'can' — which, insofar as it is relevant to the free will problem, is an excessively generalized practical ('moral') principle.

In arguing for this claim, I have attempted to discuss representative alternative views which capture significant aspects of our intuitions regarding the problem, and which do so without unnecessary complexity. One cannot, of course, survey all possible ways of dealing with such a complex and controversial issue, but one can hope to examine enough possibilities so that one may — with suitable accompanying argument — render one's own position plausible.

I should perhaps add a few words of explanation for the inclusion of the last chapter — on the relationship between God and morality — and especially of its second half. Since one central claim of the book is the denial that there are single principles determinative of the rightness of actions, it is not, I take it, inappropriate to include a brief discussion critical of the claim that God's will is constitutive of (moral) value. In fact, I try to develop an argument showing that it is self-defeating to suppose that actions are right or wrong in virtue of the subjective reaction of any agent, divine or not. If this argument succeeds — and, indeed, even if it does not, since there are *many* reasons for doubting that divine will is the criterion of moral value — the question may be raised as to what the relation *is* between God and morality. I argue that far from its being one of dependence, it is, effectively, a relation of incompatibility. This argument, in the last part of Chapter X, is rather compressed, but since it is not central to the more general argument of the book, it is probably best to leave its extended exposition to a more appropriate context. One point should be clear, however: my argument is not designed to show that the traditional problem of evil is incapable of resolution. Rather, it presupposes — not perhaps with complete plausibility — that, at one level, a positive solution to that problem has been given.

The materials of this book were presented in seminars which I gave at the University of Washington in the Spring Quarter of 1979 and in the Fall Quarter of 1981. I have obviously failed to learn as much from my students as I should have; I have some reason to believe that this failure has been reciprocated. While I must apologize for both sorts of failure, I must, more importantly, express my gratitude to all who participated in the seminars for their helpful and thought-provoking comments.

Small parts of this book have appeared elsewhere, generally in somewhat different form. Some of Chapter II appeared in 'Acrasia and Practical Reasoning', *Pacific Philosophical Quarterly* **61**, (1980); some of Chapter V in 'Responsibility and the Causation of Action', *American Philosophical Quarterly* **6** (1969); and some of Chapter X, in 'Because God Wills It', *Grazer Philosophische Studien*, **14** (1981). I should like to thank the editors of these journals for their permission to reprint these selections.

Finally, my thanks to Mary Whisner and to Katie Kocis for their help in preparing this manuscript. Not only were their considerable secretarial skills called into play, but also their deciphering abilities were severely tested.

Seattle, Washington
July 1982

CHAPTER I

INTRODUCTION

It will not have escaped the notice of the reader who has even a slight familiarity with the history of western philosophy that the items listed in the above title bear at least a superficial similarity to that famous triad which Kant took to be presupposed by practical reasoning, viz., God, freedom and immortality. Of this last notion I shall say nothing in the sequel; within the Kantian world-view, at any rate, it is so closely tied to that of God that to reject the latter as a 'postulate' of practical reasoning is, in effect, to reject the former as well. And I.shall argue below that God's existence, at least if God is conceived as a supreme personal being, far from being presupposed by practical reasoning, is, in important ways, incompatible with it. Incidentally, I should in fairness fore-warn the reader who might otherwise be misled on this point that my discussion of God and freedom has relatively little to do with Kant's particular treatment of these topics.

Of greater concern to most philosophers than the question of the bearing of God's existence on morality is that of the relevance of human freedom to the very possibility of morality: Kant used, though in different ways, an axiom often associated with his name, that 'ought' implies 'can', to argue that God – and immor-tality – as well as 'contracausal' freedom are presuppositions of morality. Few, I think, now find the arguments respecting God and immortality persuasive. But many, philosophers and others, find the argument with respect to freedom, if not persuasive, at least of sufficient force to lead to philosophical perplexity which finds expression in the following sort of question. There is a doc-trine, determinism, which holds that every event has a cause. Now

1

if determinism is true — and on Kant's view it is, at least for the world of experience — then there are sufficient conditions for a person's actions (as for every other event) which can be traced back to factors outside the agent's control. How then can the agent justifiably be held responsible for his or her[1] actions? Implicitly presupposed in that question is some version of the Kantian axiom, without some form of which it is unclear that the question of determinism — or of indeterminism — is even *relevant* to that of responsibility. Surely a critical look at this 'axiom' is in order. Such an examination will show, I believe, that 'freedom' in any sense incompatible with determinism, is not a presupposition of responsibility and of the possibility of morality.

The foregoing remarks will have sufficed to make evident the fact that I shall be dealing with versions of the Problem of Evil and of the Free Will Problem, and the reader may wonder why anyone should be concerned today about these old philosophic chestnuts. Well, one might say that there's no accounting for interests (except, of course, in terms of other interests). Or one might note that an alternative decription of 'an old philosophic chestnut' is one suggested above, namely, that of a *perennial philosophical problem*, and surely even a small step forward toward the solution of such a problem is worthwhile. And I flatter myself that I have taken such a step with respect to the two problems at issue. But more important is the bearing of the discussion of these two problems on our understanding of the nature of practical reasoning. (I shall have more to say about what I mean by this expression in the next chapter.) Partly what is involved is simply the removal of obstacles: one important obstacle to the correct appraisal of the role of moral reasoning is the still widespread belief that the existence of God or (especially) of contracausal freedom *is* a presupposition of such reasoning. It is important to argue against this belief, not only because it is false, but also because it rests on principles whose consistent application must lead to confusion and ultimately to moral skepticism.

My discussion will presuppose and at the same time illustrate a certain view of the nature of practical reasoning, a view which I shall later[2] explicitly defend. The view in question has many affinities to what is called Ethical Intuitionism. but since that very name may suggest epistemological views of a dubious sort, and since Intuitionism, like any other historical doctrine, has become inextricably associated with the specific views of those recognized as its proponents, with many of which views I disagree, I am reluctant to characterize my view as a form of Intuitionism. If I *had to* give it a name, I might call it Judgmentalism: it is fortunate, on aesthetic grounds if on no other, that I do not.

That morality is possible only on the assumption of the existence of God (cf. "Without God anything is permitted") or of free will, each conceived of in a particular way to be discussed below — is a belief which is by no means limited to theists or to libertarians. And, obviously, if an atheist believes that theism is a presupposition of morality, he will be led to moral nihilism, as will the determinist who supposes that indeterminism is such a presupposition.

To combat moral nihilism and skepticism would in itself be an adequate motive for writing this essay, but I hope that the discussion will serve more positively to shed light on the nature of practical reasoning. I wish to emphasize that this is not a treatise on Theology, Metaphysics, or the Philosophy of Science: I shall be concerned with God and Free Will only insofar as they may be thought to have relevance for practical reasoning, i.e., for rational evaluation of judgments concerning what persons should do or should have done. Thus e.g., I shall not be concerned with God as an explanatory principle — not to be sure, a tremendous loss, since a standard theological 'explanation' consists in replacing a finite problem with an infinite mystery. Nor, again, shall I be concerned with trying to determine, *a priori* or otherwise, to what extent events in the universe may be subsumable under causal laws; for purposes of practical resaoning, fortunately, such a determination will prove to be unecessary. But clearly, I cannot mention all the problems with which I shall not be concerned. Perhaps it will be more useful to indicate what I shall discuss.

In the next chapter, as I mentioned earlier, I shall explain what I mean by 'practical reasoning'. This explanation is necessary since, as will appear, my use of the expression deviates from popular and from much philosophic usage. I shall then proceed to formulate the Free Will Problem, and, in subsequent chapters, to deal with proposed solutions to it. My general claim is that the problem arises from an implicit or explicit acceptance of the Kantian axiom that 'ought' implies 'can', understood in such a way that this acceptance alone rules out the possibility of moral responsibility, or of what I shall call 'obligability', and hence of practical reasoning. Without this axiom or principle, so understood, the free will problem does not arise. But examination of the principle shows it to be itself a principle of practical reasoning, and one which is not only implausible in application, but even self-defeating. This leads me to a discussion of the role of general principles in practical reasoning, and then to an account of such reasoning which, while being an account of *reasoning*, does not involve an appeal to principles (which appear, in any event, not to be available). In the penultimate chapter I attempt to apply this account by sketching the sort of justification which one might give for the practice of holding persons responsible for their actions even in a deterministic universe. In the final chapter I argue that on the traditional conception of God, morality, far from presupposing God's existence, is incompatible with it, at least insofar as morality is concerned with issues which we must take seriously. The relevance of considerations raised in earlier chapters to this last one will, I trust, become sufficiently clear as we proceed.

CHAPTER II

PRACTICAL REASONING, ACTION, AND
WEAKNESS OF WILL

"The aim [of ethical inquiry] is, not practice, but propositions about practice; and propositions about practice are not themselves practical, any more than propositions about gases are gaseous."
— Bertrand Russell, "The Elements of Ethics"

"Perhaps acrasia is one of the best examples of a pseudo-problem in philosophical literature"
— John Lemmon, "Moral Dilemmas"

Before turning to a discussion of the venerable problem of freedom and responsibility, I should say a few words about my use of the expression 'practical reasoning'. There are judgments expressible in sentences of the form 'All things considered, [person or agent] P ought (not) to perform (have performed, be performing) [action] A'. Any such judgment I shall call a practical judgment. On this usage, it is a practical judgment, e.g., that, all things considered, Socrates ought to have escaped from jail instead of remaining and being executed, even though in an obvious sense — that, roughly, of having applicability to our everyday affairs — it is clearly not a *practical* judgment. Now by 'practical reasoning', I mean simply the presentation and weighing of reasons in support of or in opposition to a practical judgment. So construed, practical reasoning, in a given case, at least, need not be practical in the Aristotelian sense of being directed to practice: one may have a theoretical curiosity in determining whether a given action was, overall, a suitable one, whether, e.g., Socrates did the right thing in refusing the opportunity to escape. Many philosophers suggest that one's interest in practical reasoning about historical cases lies in its possible applicability to relevantly similar future cases. But the *possibility* of practical application of a bit of knowledge hardly serves to show that the knower's interest in it is (must be) practical, else there is no such thing as a theoretical interest — surely an odd view to be taken by a philosopher! This point holds especially if the inquirer sees no serious possibility of being confronted by a relevantly similar case.

I do not, of course, wish to deny that the normal point of engaging in practical reasoning is practical, i.e., that one normally tries to determine what he ought to do in order to do it. But it is no part of the *meaning* of the claim that one ought to do something that one does it, or tends to do it. The claim is simply that the action in question satisfies certain evaluative standards — including, as we shall see, standards attributing responsibility to the agent. The question of the agent's motivation to perform an action . is, on my use of 'ought' only contingently related to the correctness of the claim that he ought to perform it. I am concerned, in other words, with what Aristotle called practical 'understanding' rather than practical 'wisdom'.[1] Exclusive attention to the latter concept by Aristotle (and Plato) and subsequent moral philosophers has led to unnecessary perplexity with regard to a number of problems, but especially that of *akrasia* or weakness of will. I shall say a few words about that problem below.

Perhaps the clearest evidence of the lack of logical connection between the *concepts* of obligation[2] and motivation is provided by the not unusual case in which an agent is not aware of what he ought to do. That there are such cases is attested, *inter alia*, by the fact that we frequently try to *determine* what we ought to do. Ignorance of what we ought to do is, of course, the general Socratic explanation of why we fail to do what we ought. But this explanation leaves no room for either weakness of will or for what we consider genuine *moral* failure. (The person who 'doesn't know better' is more likely to be pitied than blamed for his actions.)

A more plausible case can be *made for* the claim that there is a logical relation between an agent's *believing* that he ought to perform a certain action and his performing it. It is not unreasonable to suppose that if I sincerely believe that, all things considered, I ought to perform some action, then, if I am not prevented from doing so, I perform the action. Now even if this supposition is correct, it is more a reflection on the logical connection between belief and action than it is on that between obligation and action or obligation and motivation. A tendency to act on a belief is one, and often the central, criterion of the belief's being (sincerely) held. This is so regardless of the content of the belief, whether, e.g., the belief concerns what we ought to do, or, say, the likelihood that a bridge will collapse, provided only that it makes sense to speak of 'acting on the belief'. But action is a criterion of an agent's holding a belief only on the supposition that the agent is motivated in a certain way. Thus, we might say that a truck-driver demonstrates his belief that a particular bridge is structurally unsound by taking a long detour to avoid it. This assumes a certain obvious normal motivation; if he were bent on suicide he might manifest the same belief by driving his truck onto the bridge.

Now although there are considerations tending to blur the distinction between belief and motivation in the case of practical judgments, it is nonetheless a distinction which common-sense morality, rightly, in my opinion, recognizes. On this view, a person may believe — may, indeed know — that a certain course of action is right and fail to pursue it, or believe that a certain action is wrong and nonetheless perform it. Indeed such descriptions would characterize the paradigmatic cases of moral failure: such failure is primarily a matter of (unexcused) improper *motivation*. Even when moral failure is the result of culpable ignorance, or of some other non-motivational factor, the *culpability* is a function of

earlier improper motivation, such as the agent's having been inade-
quately motivated to learn.

Why is the distinction between the belief that one ought to do
something and the motivation to do it often blurred, or lost,
among philosophers? In part this may be due to the failure to
distinguish two different senses or uses of the expression 'reasons
for acting'. It is a truism that insofar as the judgment or belief
that one ought to do so and so is rational it is based on reasons.
Those reasons which support or justify such a belief may be called
reasons for acting. But also those considerations which motivate
an individual to act may be called (his) reasons for acting. Now
it seems to me that we must keep these two aspects of rational
actions distinct. One aspect is the determination that a proposed
action is the one that should be performed, all things considered.
This determination involves practical reason*ing*, and the reasons
presented may be called justifying reasons.[3] I should prefer to
call them *evaluative reasons* since 'justifying' suggests reference
to just those reasons which (a) *support* a given practical conclusion, and (b) do so conclusively. That performing a certain action,
e.g., would involve breaking a promise, is an evaluative reason that
counts *against* the claim that one ought to perform the acton, and,
of course, it is not a conclusive reason. On both these counts, the
use of 'justifying' would be inappropriate. Evaluative reasons are
a subclass of probative reasons, a class which includes deductively
conclusive considerations and inductive evidence. All are considerations or reasons relevant to the acceptability of a belief or a
proposition. The second sort of reasons for acting, which Frankena
calls 'exciting reasons', are not probatively or evidentially related
to a judgment, but rather are related motivationally or causally
to an action. While the first sort of reason is used to evaluate a
claim or judgment about an action, the latter is employed to
explain an action.

It may be objected that if practical reasoning culminates in a judgment, then it is not genuinely *practical*, since reasoning properly so described must culminate in an action. One might be tempted to respond that whatever ends in an action rather than a judgment is not properly called *reasoning*, but both points are merely verbal. Practical reasoning, as I conceive it, ends in a judgment about an action; in what I have called a practical judgment. Substantive questions concern the relation between that judgment and the action prescribed or proscribed in it, and between the holding of such a judgment and that action. It seems to me that the answer to both sorts of question is that the relation is a contingent one.

It seems clear that the relationship between someone's obligation to do A and his doing A is contingent. This can be shown, as we saw above, by any case in which the agent is unaware that the preponderance of reasons – even if these be limited to reasons which he would accept – supports the claim that he ought to do A. In such a case, while it is true that he ought to do A, he may not even have a tendency to do so.

But suppose that the agent is (rationally) convinced that he ought to do A, won't he *ipso facto* be motivated to do A?[4] One may, of course, be led to an affirmative answer to this question by a confusion of evaluative and motivating reasons. The possibility that there may be (unthought of) evaluative reasons which are (therefore) inefficacious, reinforces the claim – plausible enough anyway – that there are two kinds of 'reasons for acting'. One may also be led to an affirmative answer to the question by thinking only of those cases – the standard kind – where one attempts to decide what he ought to do with a predetermined view to doing that which is so described. But here determining what one ought to do does not provide the motive for action – that was presupposed – it provides the description of the action.

Opponents of both ethical naturalism and ethical intuitionism contend that if moral or practical judgments state 'facts' then we are at a loss to account for their important relation to action. Now, as will become abundantly clear below, I do not think practical judgments are 'factual' in the sense suggested by ethical naturalism, namely that they collapse into, or are entailed by the (factual) reasons which support or justify them. Be this as it may, the 'factual' character of practical judgments does not preclude their leading to action. If one, in believing a practical judgment, believes a 'fact', namely that a given action falls under certain standards, or that the action is better supported by evaluative reasons than its alternatives, then that factual belief needs but a motivational premise — or rather a motive, that of tending to do what one believes one ought — to yield an action. And of course, given the nature of our moral training, wherein we learn moral standards and develop the tendency to act on them at the same time, this tendency, in stronger or weaker form, can be expected to appear in any socialized individual. This fact about moral training would suggest that the relation between perceived obligation and motivation, even if universally obtaining, is other than necessary. More importantly, it would show that the motivation need not be very strong, and in particular it would show that its strength need not be proportional to the strength of the belief; and it is only this sort of proportionality which would give rise to a problem of weakness of will.

Clarity about the relation of obligation and motivation requires keeping at least these three notions distinct: that of the weight of the evaluative reasons relevant to a given practical judgment (the attempt to identify and weigh these reasons is the task of what I call practical reasoning); that of the strength of the agent's belief in or acceptance of the practical judgment (insofar as this belief is rational, its strength will be a function of the agent's perception of the weight of the evaluative reasons); and that of the strength of the agent's motivation to act on the accepted belief. Recognizing the first distinction is tantamount to recognizing the distinction between an agent's obligation to perform an action and the agent's *belief* that he ought to perform the action. And surely the relation between these is contingent or 'external'.[5] And, hence, so is the relation between an agent's obligation and his motivation, since the existence of an unrecognized obligation can hardly motivate one to act. The external character of the relation between the existence of an obligation, which depends on, and only on, the existence of justifying reasons, and the agent's belief in that obligation is assured by the possibility of there being evaluative reasons which the agent has either failed to consider or which he has incorrectly assessed. Anyone not concentrating on his own decision-making process, on present tense first-person practical judgments, cannot fail, in any case, to be aware of the distinction between what an agent ought to do and what he (the agent) believes he ought to do. The point, of course, is not that *others* frequently fail to recognize their obligations, although that is true, but that in *saying* that I ought to do A, I 'imply' that I believe that I ought, and that since I am the agent or the potential agent of A, the claim that the agent ought to do A, and the agent's belief that he ought to do A become, in that circumstance, intertwined.

I may note, incidentally, that although throughout this essay I shall treat sentences of the form 'X ought to do A' as expressing propositions capable of being supported or opposed by reasons, the distinction between the claim that an agent ought to perform an action and his belief that he ought to do so does not depend on this fact. Even, for example, an extreme emotivist who holds that my saying that P ought to do A merely expresses my approval of P's doing A should say that that judgment obviously has no implications concerning the state of P's beliefs.

Finally, one might try to deny that one's obligation and one's obligation-belief are related only externally by holding that the claim that P ought to do A cannot be justified if P does not believe or realize that he ought to do A. For to say that P ought to do A

is to say that *A* falls under standards, including standards of obligability,[6] i.e., that not only is *A* the right action in the circumstances, but that *P* is rightly held responsible for *A*. The objection to claiming that *P* ought to do *A* when *P* does not realize that he ought to is that we are thereby impermissibly holding *P* responsible for the performance of an action the obligatory nature of which he is unaware. The objection trades on the fact that an agent's ignorance of relevant circumstances frequently serves to absolve him of obligability for an action or an omission, but this fact is, of course, insufficient to sustain the objection. It would do so only if ignorance of one's obligations were never *culpable* ignorance. And this is clearly not the case; one need think only of the individual who, wanting to do something, wilfully refuses to seek out or even to attend to reasons opposed to his performing the action.

We seem left with the conclusion, uninteresting in itself, that obligations and motivations are related only contingently (and, one may add, too infrequently). Perhaps those who seem to claim otherwise really intend to claim a logical connection between an agent's beliefs (or assertions — but these function, presumably, as indications of beliefs) as to what he ought to do, and his motivations. Now we have already seen a reason, based on the nature and purpose of moral training, for there to be a connection between perceived obligation and motivation to act, but this is not a logical connection. Nor, as we have remarked, does this connection give rise to the problem of weakness of will, that is, the problem of how a person can recognize what he ought to do and yet fail to do it, since even though one's believing that he ought to do *A* may provide *some* motivation for doing *A*, it provides no reason for supposing that there may not be stronger countervailing motives. To be sure, one may be, as I am, sympathetic with E. J. Lemmon's contention[7] that there *is* no genuine *problem* of weakness of will but just a fact to be recognized. But one may speculate as to why so many philosophers have thought that there is such a problem. This thought is clearly connected with the (unreasonable) demand that reason should be practical, not just in the sense of leading to judgments about action, but in the sense of leading to action. Perhaps this demand in turn arises from the classical view that while men (i.e., persons[8]) are accountable for their actions, the essence of man is rationality, and hence that reason is *necessarily* tied to actions. Whatever the source of the puzzle concerning weakness of will, however, the more important concern is to see its meaning.

It should be clear that there is a problem of weakness of will just in case the sufficient motivating reasons for a given action are equivalent to its justifying reasons, or rather to those perceived to be justifying. For if it is acknowledged that there may be reasons which are seen to be evaluative, i.e., as relevant to the questions of the act's justification, but which do not lead us to action, or that there may be motives to act which are not perceived as factors tending to justify the action, then there is simply no problem of weakness of will. In either case, we shall find unsurprising the inability of reason (even extended to include *judgments* of what ought to be done, i.e., practical judgments) to determine desire (and hence action). We may note that while both cases have regard for the relative inefficacy of practical reason with respect to desire, the former tends to point to the weakness of reason, while the latter emphasizes the strength of desire.

Any continuing concern with the problem of weakness of will is probably attributable to failure to distinguish between those 'reasons for action' which are evaluative from those which are motivational. Once the distinction is made, the attempt to hold them equivalent, as required for the existence of the problem, seems totally implausible. The (perceived) *weight* of evaluative reasons simply fails to correlate with the *strength* of motivational reasons. This is especially obvious when considerations of self-interest, especially short-run considerations, are at stake: such considerations notoriously have much greater strength than they ought, *and than we recognize they ought*. It should be superfluous to point out that there are motives, e.g., fear, or lack of courage, greed, lust, hatred, desire for revenge, which are manifested in particular motivating reasons and whose strength generally is, and not infrequently is perceived as being, utterly disproportionate to the weight of the corresponding evaluative reason. Now the strength of any motive may be disproportionate to its weight as a reason, but these motives provide examples in which motive and reason frequently do not even tend in the same *direction*: John's desire to hurt James may explain (be the motivating reason for) his hitting him, but of itself it does not tend to justify (provide a positive evaluative reason for) his doing so, and John may be aware of this at the time of his action. The distinction between motivating and evaluative reasons is perfectly familiar, and in general, moreover, there is nothing odd in their working at cross-purposes, as is particularly clear in the case of second and third person or past tense judgments. Thus, "I should have done A, but I didn't" or "He ought to do A, but he probably won't" offer no conceptual difficulties. If "I ought to do A, but I shan't" sounds odd[9] it does so, presumably, because it raises some question of the sincerity of the belief implicit in one's saying "I ought to do A": the test of one's sincerely saying that he ought to do A is his doing A when circumstances permit. But if we bear in mind the distinction of two kinds of reason for acting, then the air of paradox disappears – if, indeed, it ever existed. When one sincerely asserts that he ought to do A, he is saying, in effect, that justifying reasons – reasons which *ought* to motivate him to do A – exist, not that motivating reasons do. But it may be said that unless the agent is prepared to act on his assertion that he ought to do A by doing A, circumstances permitting, then his assertion represents mere lip-service to conventional moral standards. If 'lip-service' implies the more or less deliberate misrepresentation of one's views, then this objection has little force, for individuals frequently do things which they at least sincerely *believe* at the time they ought not to do, or fail to do things which they sincerely *feel* they ought. This sincerity of belief or feeling may be present in any sort of case, but it is probably most clear in cases involving the agent's own self-interest, in, e.g., the smoker's assertion that he ought to give up smoking. One who claims that he ought to do something which, say, conduces to preserving his health is hardly to be accused of paying lip-service to conventional standards, especially when in most sorts of circumstances he tends to act so as to maintain his health. (Even if he did not, this fact would not impugn his sincerity, although it might be very relevant to the question of his self-deception.) There are, moreover, other tests of the sincerity of one's professed practical beliefs over and above one's normal behavior patterns, tests such as the presence of feelings of remorse, regret, or guilt at the failure to act in accordance with those expressed beliefs.

Finally, one could trivialize the whole discussion of the relation between 'ought' and motivation by taking as the sole and sufficient condition of someone's believing that he ought to do A that, when circumstances permit, he does A. Such a drastic revision of what I take to be our normal conception of (perceived) obligation taken, presumably in the interest of making (practical) reasoning truly practical, would have the anomolous result of making practical reasoning superfluous: on this account whatever we did would *ipso facto* accord with our genuine standards, and indeed would be but a manifestation of them.

There are, it would appear, two distinguishable conditions on the rational and deliberate carrying out of an action, first, the agent's determination of what he ought to do, and second, the agent's desire or motivation to do that which he has determined he ought to do. To be sure, these factors need not appear in this temporal sequence, and indeed the latter normally provides a background condition of the agent's inquiry into what he ought to do. (Hence, the necessity of this condition is often overlooked.) But if the first condition is thought to include the second, then an unnecessary – and, as we have seen, ultimately absurd – restriction is placed on that which we ought to do. The untenability of this restriction is particularly evident with respect to judgments of what others ought to do (and of what we ourselves, as well as others, ought to have done). And if, as Hare and many others have claimed, 'ought' judgments are implicitly universal in character, then the lack of logical connection between obligation and motivation in third person practical judgments should hold also in the analysis of the content of first person practical judgments. Conversely, of course, one could argue that since in the first person case obligation involves motivation, it does so in other cases as well.[10] Not only is this claim implausible in itself, but it also raises, as we have just seen, serious questions about the point or even the possibility of practical reasoning.

On my view practical judgments, the concern of practical reasoning, are genuine judgments, beliefs, or propositions, and are capable of support or opposition by (probative) reasons. As with other beliefs, the acceptance of a practical judgment, even a present or future tense first-person practical judgment, leads to action only when supplemented by a desire or other motivating factor. But even if one rejects this claim, and supposes that there is a logical link between obligation and motivation, he will presumably allow for the evaluation of sentences of the form 'all things considered, P ought (not) to do (have done) A', sentences which I have spoken of as expressing practical judgments. This evaluation of practical judgments I continue to call practical reasoning even though on my view such reasoning does not of itself lead to action. I maintain this usage in part because practical reasoning will frequently occur against background conditions which *will* serve to link the result of such reasoning to action, and in part for want of a more satisfactory expression. The obvious alternative, 'moral reasoning' (as well as 'moral judgment' for the judgment of what one ought, overall, to do), suffers from its suggesting that *moral* considerations, as contrasted with, say, prudential considerations, are necessarily always overriding.[11] But to suppose that moral considerations, say considerations of justice, however trivial, must have greater weight than considerations of prudence, however urgent, seems simply false.[12]

But this is more than enough on my conception of practical reasoning, and the attempt to disentangle it from other processes which might be or have been so called.

CHAPTER III

THE DILEMMA OF OBLIGABILITY

"Evidently, however, none of these arguments are really decisive, and the position is extremely unsatisfactory to anyone with a real curiosity about such a fundamental question. In such cases it is a heuristic maxim that the truth lies not in one of the two disputed views but in some third possibility which has not yet been thought of, which we can only discover by rejecting something assumed as obvious by both the disputants."
    — Frank P. Ramsey, *The Foundations of Mathematics*

It may well be wondered whether further discussion of the free will problem can possibly be warranted. What William James wrote over nine decades ago at the beginning of his famous paper 'The Dilemma of Determinism' should hold *a fortiori* today, namely that "a common opinion prevails that the juice has ages ago been pressed out of the free-will controversy, and that no new champion can do more than warm up stale arguments which everyone has heard." James went on to say, "This is a radical mistake. I know of no subject less worn out, or in which inventive genius has a better chance of breaking open new ground. . . ." Since James wrote, the subject has gotten a good deal more 'worn out', but I believe that it still provides an instructive prolegomenon to, as well as an instructive application of, an adequate account of practical reasoning. Incidentally, I do not pretend to 'inventive genius', nor do I write as a 'new champion' of either determinism or of indeterminism — I have no idea to what extent events in the world fall under what may reasonably be accounted *causal* regularities.

Fortunately for present purposes we do not have to decide the issue between determinists and indeterminists: it would surely be catastrophic if the possibility of practical decision-making rested on our having first resolved that abstract metaphysical riddle.

In any event, the force of each view lies in great measure, as we shall see, in difficulties which it raises for the position opposed to it. These difficulties pertain to the alleged inability of the opposing view to make sense of the notion of responsibility, or, as I shall call it, obligability. Hence arises the dilemma of obligability. After having set forth this dilemma, I shall look at a number of attempts to deal with one or both of its horns. While none of these attempts strikes me as successful, almost all raise points which appear significant in light of what I take to be a satisfactory resolution of the dilemma. This resolution depends on an application of *Ramsey's maxim*, or at least on that part of the maxim which suggests our "rejecting something assumed as obvious by both the disputants". In the present case this 'something' is the claim that 'ought' implies 'can', at least insofar as this claim is thought to be relevant to the free will controversy. The mutual relevance of this discussion to the theory of practical reasoning will, I trust, become clear in the further course of this essay.

To formulate the dilemma, it will be useful to introduce two terms, and to indicate a set of possible logical relations which might be thought to hold between them. One is that of *determinism*, the doctrine that every event has a cause. For present purposes we do not require a terribly precise notion of cause: we may think of a cause of an event as a sufficient condition of the event which is logically independent of it. Ideally the description of the cause and of the effect can be subsumed under a true universal generalization of the form 'whenever an event of type C occurs, an event of type E occurs', but in practice finding suitable descriptions of cause and effect such that they can be components of such a generalization becomes difficult, if not impossible.[1] The reason for maintaining this ideal, incidentally, as well as the requirement that cause be distinct from effect, is perhaps this: one primary purpose of stating the cause of a given event is to provide an *explanation* of that event. Insofar as a putative causal explanation is not at least implicitly universal, it has an element of the *ad hoc* about it; and insofar as an explanation does not refer beyond the explanandum (the event to be explained) it is circular. But an *ad hoc* explanation or a circular explanation, if these expressions are not simply contradictions in terms, is clearly a putative explanation which is defective. In any event, this will have to suffice for the present account of causation; for anything else I shall have to rely on the reader's intuitions concerning the use of 'cause', 'law', and related terms.

The other notion is that of obligability. I borrow the term 'obligability' (and its cognates) from C. D. Broad,[2] and for reasons to be mentioned shortly, employ it instead of the more familiar 'responsibility'. In his classic paper, which provides one of the clearest statements of what I call the dilemma of obligability, Broad writes, "It will be convenient to call an action 'obligable' if and only if it is an action of which 'ought to be done' or 'ought not to be done' can be predicated."[3]

He continues:

It will be convenient to call an action substitutable if, either it was done but could have been left undone, or it was left undone but could have been done. We may then sum up the situation by saying that an action is obligable if and only if it is in a certain sense substitutable; that unless all judgments of obligation are false in principle, there are obligable actions, and, therefore, unless all judgments of obligation are false in principle, there are actions which are, in this sense, substitutable.[4]

This last point may be taken as Broad's formulation of the claim that 'ought' implies 'can'; he has entitled this section of his paper 'Obligability Entails Substitutablity'. To be sure, one may wonder about the reverse implication implicit in Broad's use of 'if and only if'; it would seem that there are trivial substitutable actions (e.g., tying one's left shoe before tying one's right shoe) which are not obligable, concerning which one does not normally make 'judgments of obligation'.

Now I propose to use 'ought' (and 'ought not') as the most general and inclusive term(s) of practical evaluation, and I adopt the term 'obligable' in part because of its explicit definitional relation to 'ought' and 'ought not', and, in part, because of what I take to be its advantages over the alternative 'responsible'.

It seems to me useful to have a pair of terms for the overall evaluation, favorable or unfavorable, of given action. But if, as I propose to do, we use 'ought' and 'ought not' for this purpose, our usage will not infrequently deviate from the ordinary. This is so largely because the terminology of practical judgment not only states the positive or negative evaluation of an action, but often indicates something of the weight of the reasons for this evaluation. Thus, we are unlikely to *say* of someone who has committed an act of extreme cruelty, "He ought not to have done that" in part, perhaps, because it would go without saying, but in part because the 'ought not' locution is simply not forceful enough for the case. Again, we are unlikely to use the expression 'ought' with respect to what we take to be an act of supererogation, because that expression suggests a connection with that which is obligatory or required. But if we bear in mind the distinction between the practical evaluation of an action, whether favorable or unfavorable, and the reasons for this 'verdict', including, of course, consideration of possible alternative actions, then the proposal to have a single pair of terms for practical evaluation will, I trust, appear less "odd". We can then accommodate the range of expressions running, e.g., from 'unspeakable' or 'totally impermissible' through 'permissible' or 'not prohibited' to 'a good thing to do', 'obligatory', and 'far beyond the call of duty' or 'supererogatory', by thinking of them not as providing just a practical evaluation, but as incorporating in addition a weighing of the reasons for that evaluation.

We shall be concerned with the expression 'ought' solely as it is used in the evaluation of actions. This use may occur in (particular) practical judgments, as, e.g., "Dr. Smith ought to have told Jones the truth about his heart condition", or in practical generalizations, such as "One ought to keep one's promises". We may note that there are many uses of 'ought' other than those involved in practical evaluation. There is the 'ought' of probable expectation ("John's plane ought to be arriving about now"), the 'ought' of desirability ('Everyone ought to be happy'), the 'ought' of pseudo-evaluation ("If you want to believe the truth then you ought to believe that p" — in effect a long-winded way of asserting that p is true.) Many 'hypothetical imperatives' are pseudo-evaluative. "If you want E you ought to do M" *may* simply state that M is an effective means to E. We may contrast this locution with "*Since* you want E, you ought to do M" where the 'ought' has evaluative force; the potential agent's desire for a certain consequence (E) of his act (M) is taken by the speaker as an evaluative reason in favor of that agent's performing the action.

It is, of course, the 'ought' of practical evaluation which is relevant to the question of persons' responsibility, and it is this use, presumably, which Broad had in mind when he introduced the notion of obligability. Here let me say why I adopt Broad's term in preference to the more common 'responsibility'. (The grounds are obviously not aesthetic.) To be sure 'responsible', in the sense of the term with which we are concerned, is applied to agents — they are 'responsible for' their actions — and 'obligable', as introduced by Broad is applied to actions. I propose to apply the latter term to persons — to say that they are 'obligable for' their actions, as well as to these actions. The reasons for this extension, in addition to the definitional linkage between 'obligable' and 'ought' have to do with the fact that 'responsible' is at once too broad and too narrow for our purposes. It is too broad, in that in a sense to attribute responsibility for a state of affairs is merely to attribute causal efficacy for its occurrence. (Cf. "The lack of snowfall last winter was responsible for this summer's water shortage.") In this sense, persons or their actions may be responsible for states of affairs for which they are not obligable, i.e., subject to moral evaluation. Any case in which a person brought about an unfortunate state of affairs as a result of non-culpable ignorance would be an instance. It may be too narrow, in that (if Ryle is right) a person is normally held 'responsible' for actions which are untoward, or which tend to be blameworthy.[5] The use of 'obligable' is not so restricted — the term is applicable whenever the question of practical evaluation, positive or negative, arises. And of course, in the context of the free-will problem, the question arises as to how persons are justifiably to be held blameworthy or praiseworthy for their actions, i.e., how agents can justifiably be accounted obligable.

This problem of free will may be viewed as one involving the logical relationship between determinism and obligability, or rather between the doctrine of determinism and the claim that we are obligable for at least some of our actions. We may, for short, call this claim the obligability claim. Now, obviously, determinism may be compatible with the obligability claim or it may be incompatible with it. Those who hold the two views to be incompatible, and maintain that determinism is true (and hence that the obligability claim is false) are commonly called 'hard determinists'.[6] Those who hold the views to be incompatible, and insist that the obligability claim is true (and, therefore, that determinism is false) are often called 'libertarians'. 'Soft determinists' are those who hold determinism to be true, but compatible with the obligablity claim. I know of no name for indeterminists who maintain this compatibility position. Most indeterminists who are especially concerned with the free-will problem (as opposed to those whose indeterminism is based, e.g., on considerations derived from quantum mechanics) seem driven to their view by arguments designed to show the incompatibility of determinism and the obligability claim. Finally, we may note that *indeterminism* (the denial of determinism) may be incompatible with the obligability claim. Soft determinists, at least from Hume on, have attempted to bolster their position by claiming that the two views *are* incompatible, that the obligability claim is true and entails or presupposes determinism.

Two of these general claims taken together constitute what I call the dilemma of obligability: the claim that determinism is incompatible with obligability and the claim that indeterminism is incompatible with obligability. Clearly if both these claims are true then "obligability is a delusive notion, which neither has nor can have any application."[7] Since this conclusion has more than a bit of an air of paradox about it, a point to which I shall return below, we should be well advised to look at the arguments supporting each of the horns of the dilemma. This task will be begun in a sketchy manner here, with more detail being added as we proceeed to examine a number of counter-arguments, counter-counter-arguments, etc. As long as we maintain as axiomatic the form of the claim that 'obligability entails substitutability' the dilemma will, on my view, remain unresolved; without that claim the dilemma has no plausibility. Hence the concerned reader may take some heart in my (as yet unsupported) assurance that the 'obvious' claim does not stand up to scrutiny.

I have suggested above that most of the force of the libertarian's claim that some events, and in particular some human actions or choices, are uncaused arises from the belief that determinism, and, again, in particular the causation of human choices and actions, would render impossible or logically absurd the practice of holding people obligable for their actions. The argument here is quite familiar. Determinism, the doctrine that every event has a cause, entails that every human action is subject to causal law. But if this is so, "there will be for any action a set of sufficient conditions which can be traced back to factors outside the control of the agent".[8] But presumably, if this is so, the agent could not have done otherwise (his action is not substitutable) and hence the notions of ought and ought not do not apply (his action is not obligable). This argument is not only familiar, it is very powerful. If we add to it the not unreasonable contentions that acceptance of the obligability claim is, if nothing more, a matter of practical necessity, and that the doctrine of determinism is at best a heuristic maxim and at worst a mere metaphysical prejudice, we have a seemingly complete and reasonable answer to the question of the relation of determinism and obligability — the answer of the libertarian.

Now the determinist is not without replies to the libertarian argument — we shall look at some shortly — but it is not these that render libertarian satisfaction premature. It is rather that the question of this relation is only partly answered, indeed only partly asked.[9] For unless indeterminism and the obligability claim are consistent, the libertarian position is itself untenable. But that they are not thus consistent is the contention which constitutes the second horn of the dilemma of responsibility.

The familiar classical arguments for the incompatibility of indeterminism and obligability are perhaps neither as perspicuous nor as persuasive as those for the first half of the dilemma. This is so because they involve the assumption which is not perhaps immediately acceptable at the level of common sense that the only alternative to causal determination is sheer randomness or chance. Given this assumption the argument proceeds by the assertion that if an action (or choice, or whatever) is not the effect of antecedent causes, then its occurrence is purely a matter of chance, and clearly for such a chance occurrence the agent is not obligable. Hence to whatever extent indeterminism were to hold, to that extent the obligability claim would not. I shall return to this point shortly.

Generally, as we have seen, those espousing this sort of argument have been soft determinists; and they have sprinkled their account with considerations designed to show the regularity and/or the predictability of human actions, but these are, strictly, irrelevant to the compatibility question, however relevant they may be to the question of the truth of determinism. It is important to keep the question of the truth or falsity of determinism separate from that of the compatibility of determinism or of indeterminism with the obligability claim. The latter question is surely more likely to be reasonably decidable; in any case, it is the only question with which I shall be concerned. And since *I* take it that the answer to the question of compatibility between the obligability claim and either determinism or indeterminism is affirmative (because the argument for incompatibility in either case rests on the same untenable premise), I suppose that for purposes of an account of practical reasoning we need not pursue the further question of the truth-value of determinism.

To be sure, the compatibility claim seems supported at times by soft determinists' holding that determinism and the obligability claim are both obviously true,[10] and hence that the two doctrines *must be* compatible. But the truth of determinism is not obvious, at least not obviously so. It is, after all, a grand claim, namely that *every* event (or, to bypass one obvious difficulty, every macroscopic event) falls under a causal law. This is surely not a matter of logical necessity.[11] "But science demands it", or "The world would be unintelligible without it" — both these common claims seem simply false: explanation in terms of (non-deterministic) statistical generalizations *may* be the best attainable in certain areas. Of course, we may prefer deterministic laws as explanatory principles, but there is no guarantee that our preferences will be satisfied; if the world is fully intelligible only under the supposition of determinism, then the world may simply be less than fully intelligible. If our scientific method is made to incorporate a certain belief about the way the world is or must be, then there's madness in that method. Determinism may be a perfectly good heuristic maxim, but to suppose that its application must yield success is a bit of wishful thinking not totally unlike some of the 'practical proofs' of the existence of God.

Returning to the second horn of our dilemma, that which asserts the incompatibility of indeterminism and the obligability claim, we had seen the argument for this assertion which is based on the supposition that the only alternative to the causal determination of actions or of choices is their chance occurrence. Now most libertarians reject this supposition, but since at least one[12] does not, it will be useful to explain why the supposition of decisions or actions being merely random or chance events appears incompatible with those events being obligable. It will be useful particularly since I shall be able to show thereby that the rationale for that claim involves the same principle as is involved in the first half of our dilemma, namely, that an action is not obligable if there is for that action "a set of sufficient conditions which can be traced back to factors outside the control of the agent". It will appear that in the case of a random or chance decision or action this condition is satisfied in a trivial way. We may construe a *random* event as one for which there are no sufficient conditions outside itself. Thus, if there is a random action, it is, trivially, a sufficient condition of itself, which, as random, is outside the control of everyone, and *a fortiori* outside the control of its agent. Similarly, if, making a simplifying assumption, we suppose a random decision to be the sufficient condition of an action, then tracing back the sufficient condition of the action to the decision, we have traced it back to a factor outside the control of an agent (or, again, of anyone else). Hence, if either action, or the decision to act on which it is based, occurs as a matter of chance, then, on the supposition in question, the action is not obligable.

So far we have developed the dilemma of obligability to this point: Given a certain *prima facie* plausible supposition about an action's not being obligable if there are sufficient conditions for the action which result from factors outside the agent's control (henceforth, I shall call this the OES — Obligability Entails Substitutability — Supposition), it appears that determinism is incompatible with obligability. Moreover, if indeterminism is equated with the view that random or chance events occur, then indeterminism, too, appears incompatible with obligability. In the next chapters, we shall look at some counter-arguments of determinists and at some indeterministic views which take uncaused actions or decisions to be other than chance events. I shall argue that given the OES Supposition, none of these considerations will provide a way out of our dilemma. Thus, in the end, we shall investigate the OES Supposition, and find in its inadequacies the resolution of our dilemma. But the supposition is so attractive that it can be set aside only as a last resort — hence the necessity of the preliminary discussions, many of which I fear are boringly familiar.

So seductive is the OES Supposition, indeed, that being convinced of the truth of both horns of the dilemma of obligability (or — as in the case of hard determinists, being convinced of the truth of determinism as well as of that of the first horn of the dilemma) we may be tempted to abandon the obligability claim rather than the supposition, a temptation to which not a few, including as we have seen, C. D. Broad, succumbed. I suggest, however, that it is a temptation that we must resist.

Broad concluded his paper setting forth what I call the dilemma of obligability by writing: "It is therefore highly probable that the notion of categorical obligability is a delusive notion, which neither has nor can have any application".[13] I shall not comment

here on Broad's use of the Expressions 'highly probable' and
'categorical obligability', except to remark that the former, as
a reasonably careful reading of the passage will show, is not to
be taken too seriously, and that the latter, which Broad uses
in contrast to 'comparative obligability', appears because of
Broad's explicit but unargued assumption that "if any action
were categorically obligable, it would have to be categorically
substitutable",[14] an assumption which is, in effect, denied by
some determinists who propose a hypothetical analysis of substitutability (i.e., of "x could have done otherwise"). I shall
discuss such an analysis in the next chapter. For now, I wish
merely to consider Broad's conclusion which states in effect that
the expressions 'ought' and 'ought not' unmodified by 'ifs' have
and can have no application. Now this is quite an unacceptable
conclusion — and I do not mean simply one that is undesirable.
For, in the first place, it is clear that we frequently make judgments of the form 'X ought (not) to do (have done) so and so'
where the 'ought' or 'ought not' is intended quite categorically,
i.e. neither in Kant's 'hypothetical' nor in Broad's 'comparative'
sense. Hence, on one obvious use, categorical obligability does
have (and *a fortiori* can have) *application*. Of course, it will be
said, the claim is that obligability has no *correct* application.
But if this claim is to be taken seriously at the practical level,
it translates into the claim (or the recommendation) that while
'ought' and 'ought not' are in fact used, they ought not to be.
And this statement, however it is analyzed, is to say the least
infelicitous, if not absurd.

At a practical level, moreover, it seems obvious that we cannot
abandon the use of the notion of obligability: it is simply much
too fundamental and pervasive a feature of the life of human
beings. And if we cannot, then on the OES supposition, the
question of whether we should or not cannot arise. And if it be
claimed that abandoning the use of obligability is not impossible,

or in any case is a mere practical impossibility to which the OES supposition does not apply, we should without stopping to argue this point remember that the conclusion that no action is obligable is based in part on the premise that no action is or can be substitutable. But, on this premise, our actions in holding our actions and those of others obligable are themselves not obligable, i.e., the question of whether or not we ought to use 'ought' cannot reasonably be raised, and not because of a mere verbal infelicity involved in the question "ought we to say 'ought'?"

It would not be surprising that the dilemma of obligability should emerge as a conceptual shambles. After all, unless whatever criterion of obligability we employ is to be arbitrary, it must generalize over instances which embody distinctive instances of *prima facie* obligability as opposed to *prima facie* non-obligability — a fact obviously not restricted to the criterion of *obligability*. For present purposes we need not discuss the obvious chicken-egg question of priorities arising with respect to criteria and instances. This is not a 'paradigm case' sort of conception based on the argument that since those instances on which the criterion is based are *ipso facto* paradigm cases of the concept in question there must be such cases. There is simply too much flexibility in the relations between generalization and instances to support any claim stronger than one to the effect that the 'paradigm cases' are *prima facie* instances of the given concept. But this itself is a sufficiently strong claim to raise serious questions when we are confronted with the contention that a given concept has no (possible) application, especially when the concept is as familiar, pervasive, and seemingly ineluctable as that expressed by 'ought' and 'ought not'. It would seem *prima facie* likely in case such a claim is made that we have mistaken the nature of the criteria for the application of the concept. Among other things, then, we shall have to look at the criteria we actually employ for the application of the concept of obligability.

CHAPTER IV

WAS FREE WILL A PSEUDO-PROBLEM?

If we cannot be satisfied with the conclusion that "the notion of obligability is ... delusive,"[1] then it appears that we are well advised to examine the premises leading to this conclusion. In this chapter I propose to look at some standard responses given by determinists and some given by indeterminists in an attempt to avoid this conclusion. I shall discuss some typical and important views, but I shall make no claim of inclusiveness. I trust, however, that by the end of the next chapter, in which I discuss a recently fashionable attempt to bypass the determinism-indeterminism dichotomy, I shall have made a sufficiently persuasive case for my claim that it is the OES supposition that is the principal obstacle to the acceptance of the obligability claim. Even, however, if I fail to make such a case, I shall still try to show that the OES supposition has only a *prima facie* plausibility, and that should it finally appear that one must choose between the supposition that 'ought' implies 'can' and the claim that 'ought' and 'ought not' have application, it is clearly rational to opt for the latter.

Most attempts to show the compatibility of determinism and obligability are indebted to Hobbes and to Hume, and, indeed, are largely variations on themes set forth by these writers (often, to be sure, with a good deal of subtle refinement). Some of the principal themes (or variations) are that opponents of compatibilism fail to recognize the distinction between causation and compulsion (or between natural law and positive law), fail to see that the sort of substitutability needed for obligability is hypothetical rather than categorical, and misconstrue the (pragmatic) point of assessing obligability, namely, as a basis for the modification of behavior. Thus, the function of judgments of obligability as part of a system of morality is to further the process of encouraging desirable behavior and discouraging undesirable behavior. On this view, obligability is not only compatible with determinism, but presupposes it, or at least presupposes that human action (as modifiable) is subject to causal factors.

While I think none of these responses adequate, each does raise a point of some significance. The claim that opponents of determinism confuse causation and compulsion (in part, perhaps, because the term 'necessity' is used in connection with both) seems not without historical justification. Insofar as such confusion gives rise to a picture of determinism as involving a Jamesian 'block-universe', or as otherwise making human agents the mere victims of forces totally out of their control, then it is a confusion worth pointing out. After all, determinists think of human beliefs and human desires as causal factors, and it is surely of practical importance to distinguish an action involving such factors from occurrences happening contrary to our desires or from actions which we are compelled to perform under duress. The latter two sorts of causation rule out the possibility of free action, but determinism clearly does not entail that they are the only sorts of actions in which humans engage. And merely for purposes of assessing obligability the distinction between the first sort of case and the latter two is usually of importance, as it is for the question of 'freedom'. But what is quite unclear is how the distinction of compulsion and causation is supposed to give rise to substitutability, i.e., how it is supposed to help with *our* problem — apart, of course, from the further claim that the relevant notion of substitutability is that of hypothetical substitutability. Before turning to that more fundamental claim, it may be useful to say a bit more about the compulsion-causation distinction.

Many times the distinction is defended on the basis of a Humean or positivistic 'constant conjunction' analysis of causation which holds, in effect, that since all that is observable in the case of a causal relation between events is a uniformity of sequence between events of those kinds, this is what causality consists in. There is no point in trying to show here all — or indeed any — of what is wrong with this sort of analysis. For present purposes it suffices to point out that we have a *contrast* between causation so analyzed and compulsion only if the latter is analyzed on similar principles. And it appears that what such an analysis would yield would be the remark that, e.g., all that is observable in a given case is A's holding a pistol to B's head, *followed by* B's handing his wallet to A, and hence that such a succession of events is all that compulsion consists in. Apart from the fact that such a characterization of compulsion is clearly inadequate, it is also one that fails to yield a contrast between compulsion and causation. (This last point is not itself necessarily a defect: compulsion should be contrasted with causation not as being different from it but only as being a sub-class of it.)

In any event, the contrast between causation and compulsion will not serve to allay all concern about causation and obligability, since, after all, some causation which does not involve compulsion does serve to remove obligability. Thus a person hurled through a window by a violent explosion is not responsible for the window's breaking, even though its breaking would not have occurred had he stopped in mid-air. And, obviously, his failure to perform this action has a (merely) causal explanation.[2] Moreover, in a standard case of compulsion, there appears to be a greater degree of substitutability than in such a case of causation — one could, e.g., have decided to be shot rather than to hand over his wallet. This case suggests that compulsion acts on us via our desires, but, of course, it is not just having our desires under the control of other agents which renders our actions involuntary. The same result may occur when our desires are controlled by natural forces. Although Aristotle is in some hesitation on the matter, *we* should not

FERNALD LIBRARY
COLBY-SAWYER COLLEGE
NEW LONDON, N.H. 03257

call the action of the ship's captain in jettisoning his cargo in a
storm to save the ship voluntary. This example, incidentally,
throws doubt on the acceptability of Donald Davidson's cryptic
comment on the problem of determinism and obligability at the
end of his well-known paper 'Actions, Reasons, and Causes':

Some causes have no agents. Primary among these are those states and changes
of states in persons which, because they are reasons as well as causes, make
persons voluntary agents.[3]

The states and changes of states to which Davidson refers, are,
of course, certain desires and beliefs. The relation between the
causation-compulsion distinction, and the more subtle claim of
Davidson seems evident. Both suffer, in my judgment, from the
attempt to set forth a single principle of obligability, apparently
an instance of what Wittgenstein called 'the craving for generality'.

I remarked above that in a normal case one is obligable if he
acts as he desires, and that this is the significance of the compulsion-causation distinction (since one is generally *not* obligable
when he acts contrary to his desires, i.e., when he is forced to act).
But the question of substitutability is a separate question from
that of obligability, or rather, it ought to be separate if lack of
substitutability is supposed to be a genuine reason for absence of
obligability (more on this point below). Now if the existence of
sufficient causal conditions for an event rules out the possibility
that the event could have happened otherwise than it did — and
if it doesn't, the notion of non-substitutability will have precious
little application — then on a determinist account no event, and
a fortiori no action, is substitutable. Hence, if as appears, some
actions are obligable, determinists may be well advised to recon-
sider the supposition that obligability entails substitutability.

But there are difficulties with this line of argument connected
with a certain looseness in the notion of substitutability, or with
the use of the expression '*X* could have done otherwise'. Not

infrequently, as I have suggested elsewhere[4] this expression is used with the sole function of assigning obligability; and its denial is used to absolve of obligability. On this use, what appears to be a claim of substitutability is, in fact, one of obligability. But obviously this use, while quite common, is, for present purposes uninteresting, since it is a use which is irrelevant to the practically important claim that a showing of non-substitutability provides a reason sufficient to justify a claim of non-obligability. For, on this use, obligability and substitutability are, in effect, identified, and, on pain of circularity, the presence or absence of one can hardly be adduced as a justification for the presence or absence of the other.

Of greater importance for our problem is a claim often explicitly made by soft determinists about the concept of substitutability, namely, that it should be given a hypothetical analysis. On such an analysis, in which 'X could have done otherwise' is equated with 'X would have done otherwise, if ____ ' it appears that substitutability is compatible with determinism. Of course, it must not be forgotten that the notion of substitutability must also be so analyzed as to be relevant to the claim that obligability entails substitutability. This last point is of importance for the first difficulty which confronts a proposed hypothetical analysis of 'X can (could) do otherwise', namely what is to replace the blank in 'X does (will do, would have done) if ____ ', such that the analysis is adequate, i.e., so that the hypothetical expression is equivalent to the statement about ability, and also is relevant to the considerations of determinism and of obligability. Whether or not there is any analysis that satisfies these conditions, it is clear that not every hypothetical analysis will. Suppose, for example, that someone were to propose an analysis involving a hypothesis making reference to the composition of the agent's body which yielded such equivalences as 'he could have walked on water' and 'he would have walked on water if his bones had

been made of cork'. Such an analysis would be patently inadequate (and irrelevant); it employs the wrong kind of hypothesis.
For one thing, even on the hypothesis, the agent, lacking suitable
opportunity or motivation, would not have walked on water.
But even if the hypothesis were revised to state a sufficient condition for the action, we should not suppose, given the inclusion
of the counterfactual supposition concerning the agent's bodily
composition, that he *could* have walked on water. Hence, since
the claim contained in the expression to be analyzed would be
false, and that in the analysis true, the two are obviously not
equivalent.

One does not need such an absurd case to show that not every
replacement in the blank following 'if' will yield an inadequate
analysis. In fact, it is clear that this hypothetical expression must
contain a reference to the agent's motivation or effort. This is
clear because if 'X can ϕ' is equivalent to 'X does ϕ if _____ ' then
'X can ϕ and _____ ' states a sufficient (and necessary) condition
of 'X does ϕ', and there is no plausible general characterization
of sufficient conditions of action which makes no reference to
the agent's motives. This fact fits in well with the determinists'
proposal for a hypothetical analysis of substitutability, since as
we have remarked above, and will have occasion to discuss below,
considerations of motivation and of effort do have an important
bearing on assessments of obligability.

But there are serious difficulties, mostly quite familiar, still
confronting the analysis of 'can (do otherwise)'. The first has
to do with the verb following the 'if' in the proposed *analysans*.
It is, we have seen, to be a verb indicative of effort or motivation.
But none seems to work. Consider 'try', for example: 'X can ϕ'
is to be equated with 'X ϕ's if he tries'. It has often been remarked
that there are all sorts of actions which a person of normal abilities
commonly does and hence can do, which require no effort. Hence,
to such actions, e.g., talking and walking, and indeed most of what

we do every day, the notion of *trying* seems to have no application.[5] This might seem a trivial point about usage, which could
be remedied by introducing new terminology, but it points to a
serious difficulty in the project of the hypothetical analysis.
The difficulty is this. One might suppose that if, as in the present
case, an equivalence is suggested between a categorical statement
and a hypothetical one, a case in which the condition expressed
in the antecedent of the hypothetical statement is not satisfied
would be not a falsifying instance, but simply an irrelevant one.
Yet, intuitively, the cases in which the condition of trying are not
satisfied seem to falsify the analysis. In defense of the intuition
one might say that the analysis is supposed to be completely
general, and to apply to all actions. On the analysis some verb
of motivation/effort is supposed to specify a condition which,
together with the agent's ability is sufficient for the agent's
acting. But unless – *per impossibile* – the agent's being able to
do something is a sufficient condition of his doing it, then on the
analysis, the motivational component is a necessary condition
of the action. This is the fact which underlies our intuitions, and
is, anyway, obvious enough. It is also important. For if having
suitable motivation is a necessary condition of an action, then
if there are any unmotivated actions, the analysis fails. But if
the notion of effort/motivation is attenuated to overcome this
possibility, then it will obviously be much too weak a notion
to yield in the general case a sufficient condition for action (given
ability). The situation, in other words, is this: we are looking
for a suitable term with which to replace the blank in 'X ϕ's
if he _____ ', such that the whole is equivalent to 'X can ϕ', where
'ϕ' itself can be replaced by the description of any action. There
are some actions which a person can perform only with the
expenditure of tremendous effort. To include reference to these
actions in our formula we may be tempted to use an expression
like 'try'. (We should really need, for some cases, a locution

like 'tries as hard as he *can*', an unfortunate addition for a proposed analysis of 'can'; also, for cases involving *delicacy* of action,
of various sorts, trying as hard as one can may constitute 'trying
too hard', and interfere with success.) But since on the analysis
being able and trying would now be sufficient conditions for
doing, in those cases not involving trying (and *a fortiori* those
cases not involving trying extremely hard) it would appear that
having the ability to do ϕ would alone constitute a sufficient
condition for doing ϕ, and this is patently absurd. If, on the
other hand, one sufficiently weakens the motivation/effort condition to assure that it be a necessary condition of every action,
then on this account, anyone who is weakly motivated to do ϕ,
or puts out a meager effort to ϕ, and fails, will thereby show that
he is unable to ϕ, and this, too is absurd.

Suppose that we paper over this difficulty, not by a disjunctive
formula, which would yield only the weakest condition, but by
using a 'weasel word' indicative of a *suitable* level of motivation/
effort. For the sake of the argument let me to use the word
'desire'. So our analysis becomes 'X can ϕ' is equivalent to 'X
ϕ's if X desires to ϕ', where the latter expression is to mean
roughly 'X ϕ's if X is *suitably* motivated to ϕ and (thus) X makes
a *suitable* effort to ϕ'.

Still, difficulties abound. One is that, in a perfectly familiar
sense of 'can', it may be true that X *can* ϕ, and that X desires
(in our artificial sense) to ϕ, but that X doesn't ϕ because, to use
another blanket term, he lacks the opportunity.[6] Perhaps we
can remedy this difficulty as Nowell-Smith suggests by speaking
of an 'all-in' sense of 'can', which combines the notions of ability
and opportunity. Still, one might have the ability, the opportunity,
and the desire to ϕ, and not ϕ because of a particular lack of
knowledge. Thus, for example, a prisoner may fail to escape
because of a failure to realize that his cell door is unlocked, or
that pushing a button to which he has ready access will cause

the door to open. Now we could try to incorporate this sort of knowledge-consideration into our concept of what is intended by 'can', but not only would such an attempt be utterly lacking in plausibility, it would also undermine — by rendering trivial — our project of providing an *analysis* of 'can'. Such a project must surely presuppose at least that we don't alter the concept to be analyzed whenever a proposed analysis runs into difficulty. Again, it is worthwhile pointing out that there is a kind of context in which possession of such knowledge may be thought of as a necessary condition of saying 'X can ϕ', the kind of context in which the question of X's obligability (perhaps, say, X's blameworthiness) has been raised. But in such a context the question of whether X can ϕ *is* simply the question of whether X is obligable for (not) ϕing, and hence if this usage embodied a special *sense* of 'can', it would be a sense which is irrelevant to the claim that: X *could* not have done otherwise provides a justification for the claim that X was not obligable.

Another difficulty with the hypothetical analysis of 'can' is that there are all sorts of things which one *can* do, such as sinking a putt (Austin), hitting a home run, writing a decent sonnet, or constructing a novel proof, for which possessing this ability and suitable desire do not constitute sufficient conditions. Henry Aaron has the ability to hit home runs, but he doesn't hit a home run whenever he tries. Nor, as this sort of example illustrates, can 'X can do ϕ' be analyzed as 'he usually succeeds if he tries'[7] — in hitting home runs, as in deriving novel theorems, occasional success is all that is needed to show the relevant sort of ability: To be sure, failure to succeed in a given case will not normally be blameworthy, and so these sorts of cases are relevant to our overall problem only insofar as we are concerned with the attempt to give a general analysis of 'X can ϕ'. But the attempt to give an analysis seems of philosophic interest only as it is subordinated to a philosophic problem.

Before abandoning consideration of the hypothetical analysis, however, we should at least mention what is perhaps the central difficulty which confronts it, insofar as it is construed as a way of avoiding the determinist horn of our dilemma. The difficulty can be represented as raising the question of the *relevance* for this end of such an analysis, although since the question arises in virtue of the fact that the antecedent of the *analysans* is necessarily contrary to fact it points to a further question as to the *adequacy* of the proposed hypothetical analysis.[8] Suppose that we allow that had an individual's desire in a given case been different, he would have acted differently from the way he did in fact act. How, if his desire *could not* have been different from what it was, is this supposition any more relevant to the question of the person's obligability than is, say, the fact that had his bones been made of cork, he might have walked on water? And, of course, if determinism is true, his desire, given its causal antecedents, could not but have arisen (and similarly, in turn for these causal antecedents, their causal antecedents, and so on). This recurring worry, to which determinism gives rise, is one to which we shall return. For now, we may drop consideration of it, and of the hypothetical analysis of 'can': it seems doubtful that any such analysis can be successful, or that if it were, that it would be relevant to the problem of determinism and obligability.

If our second theme involves an attempt to resolve the *prima facie* conflict between determinism and obligability by a reinterpretation of the concept of substitutability, our third theme may be thought of as attempting this resolution by means of a new way of looking at the concept of obligability. This third theme emphasizes what is indeed an important consideration — the utilitarian or pragmatic role of the set of practices and institutions of which the practices and institutions of which the practice of assessing obligability is a component. But it overgeneralizes this role by, in effect, equating obligability with amenability to a change of behavior through the force of real or anticipated rewards or punishments; in other words, [obligability] simply consists in corrigibility — a view that not only is compatible with determinism but presupposes it.[9]

Now I am not concerned with the claim that such a view of obligability *presupposes* determinism — a claim which appears rather incautious, in that the fact that a certain class of events (obligable actions) is subject to a kind of causal influence (expected rewards or punishments) hardly shows that *every* event is caused. But, allowing that obligability as described is compatible with determinism (thereby ignoring questions pertaining to the obligability of those establishing the sanctions and concentrating exclusively on those whose actions are subject to reinforcement), we may raise the question of the adequacy of this conception of obligability. Taking our ordinary conception of obligability as a standard, this one seems clearly deficient, since there are actions which are not on this standard obligable, but which are subject to positive or negative reinforcement, e.g. those of non-human animals and of children below the age of reason [10] as well as actions which *are* thus obligable, but not subject to the causal influence of reward or punishment, e.g., those performed in the remote past.[11] To be sure one could say that we ought to abandon our ordinary conception of obligability in favor of the one under consideration, but it is hard to know what sense to make of such a recommendation, unless, perhaps, it is intended as some sort of threat! A further point, and one to which we shall return below, is that acceptance of a pure reinforcement conception of obligability involves treating persons as patients rather than as agents.

I have said enough to indicate my dissatisfaction with some of the major attempts to show the compatibility of determinism and obligability. So far, I am in essential agreement with, e.g., Campbell. But now we should look at Campbell's attempt to deal

with the other horn of the dilemma of obligability. This attempt
relies on an appeal to the notion of 'contra-causal freedom', the
existence of which, on Campbell's view, can be determined only
by an act of introspection. It is, I take it, this last epistemic claim
which is responsible for Campbell's use of the expression 'pseudo-
problem' in the title of his paper, since Campbell supposes that
positivists would find introspection an unacceptable principle
of verification, and anything whose existence had to be certified
by it unverifiable, and hence 'its' description meaningless. One
need not be a positivist, or even a fellow-traveler of positivism,
however, to find reliance on introspecting the *non-existence* of a
cause as the basis for an account of obligability (or of anything
else) a rather desperate move. As, e.g., Mill long ago pointed out,
that an event is not subsumable under a causal law is simply not
the sort of fact that one can learn by immediate inspection, either
sensory or introspectional. It seems clear that Campbell is led to
positing the need for contra-causal freedom as a condition of
obligability by being convinced that determinism is incompatible
with obligability. In fact, quite early in the paper he writes that
"the admission of unbroken causal continuity entails a *further*
admission which is directly incompatible with moral responsibility;
viz. the admission that no man could have acted otherwise than
he in fact did".[12] He goes on to say that if an analysis of obligability can be given such that obligability and determinism are
compatible, then there is 'no problem of "Free Will" in the
traditional sense'. Having proceeded to criticize a number of
attempts to provide such an analysis, he then suggests his own
positive account.

Now it is with a criticism of this positive account, an instance
of one important way of attempting to deal with one horn of
our dilemma, that I am especially concerned. In particular, I
am not concerned to discuss the question of whether or not
free will is a 'pseudo-problem'. The use of the past tense in this

chapter's title is a (need I explain?) facetious commentary on the use of this latter expression, which like the battle cries of many other failed revolutions, is no longer on everyman's lips. It was, after all, employed as a technical term in an early stage of logical positivism (recall: "A *pseudo-problem* is a problem the answer to which is not known in Vienna"). Whether free will is a pseudo-problem in the technical sense (or senses) of proponents of the Verifiability Principle is hardly a question to spark present day philosophic interest. Even Campbell did not seriously discuss that question. But if, as some of Campbell's remarks suggest, the logical compatibility of obligability and determinism suffice to show that free will is a pseudo-problem as *he* understands the term, then I think the answer to his famous question is *yes*. This is one point of my overall argument.

For the present let us see how Campbell's positive account fares. Let us overlook certain epistemological and metaphysical difficulties with the account — difficulties, e.g. with the possibility of knowing (by introspection!) that an event is uncaused, or with the possibility of there *being* a *tertium quid,* such as is demanded by Campbell's 'libertarian' account, between events which are causally determined and events which happen by 'pure chance'.[13] From the point of view of one interested in practical reasoning it will be more instructive to disregard such problems and to question the adequacy of the libertarian account simply as an account of obligability. The libertarian account of human action is offered as an alternative to both the determinist and the indeterminist accounts, each of which Campbell considers — for reasons which are familiar — incompatible with obligability or moral responsibility. By an *indeterminist* account, Campbell means one which takes pure chance as the only alternative to causation. Accepting determinists' arguments that an indeterminist account of human action would fail to account for its general predictability and regularity, Campbell allows that most human action *is* causally determined. A view which he overlooks, namely that human action, though explicable and surely not simply a result or a manifestation of pure chance is nonetheless not *causally* explicable, is one which we shall consider in the next chapter. On Campbell's account desires and inclinations are *causal* factors, and any behavior which occurs on the basis of the agent's strongest desire is, therefore, causally determined (and not obligable). In almost every case, agents act on their strongest desires; hence, the high degree of regularity in the field of human action. But, on occasion, a conflict arises between an agent's strongest desire and his duty, between what he most wants to do and what he believes (knows?) he ought to do. This contrast bears an obvious resemblance to the Kantian distinction of inclination and respect (for the moral law), and is subject to many of the same difficulties. Kant's attempt to deal with these difficulties led him to develop a 'two-worlds' (noumenal-phenomenal) account of human freedom and human action. Leaving aside theoretical difficulties with such an account such as that of identifying a given noumenal self with a particular phenomenal self – and, of course this difficulty is exacerbated on the Kantian account in which only phenomena can be meaningfully brought under the categories, so that it would make no sense to speak of *causal* relations between noumenal and phenomenal selves, or even of a continuing noumenal self, since such continuity would presuppose the category of substance – such difficulties being waived for the sake of argument, the freedom of a postulated noumenal self can be of no interest to any of us who are concerned with flesh and blood (phenomenal) persons, beings with whom we can – at least in principle – interact.

Now, both 'strongest desire' and 'duty' are, taken as capable of conflicting, forms of motivation, and as such both could be described under the rubric of desire, with 'duty' short for 'the desire to do what one (thinks he) ought'. And if a person's 'strongest desire' means, as it appears on Campbell's account to mean, that desire on which the person acts, then if one does something because he thinks he ought to do it, he is in that case (too) acting on his strongest desire. To be sure, we often distinguish between instances in which we do something because we want to, and those in which we do something because we think we ought to. But this is by no means a useful distinction for Campbell's case. Indeed, insofar as Campbell is proposing an account of *free* action, the distinction in many cases tells against his case. To do something because one is obligated or duty-bound to do it is surely not to do it more *freely* than to do it because one *wants* to; to say that a woman totally devotes herself to her husband's interests because she feels she ought to do so is hardly to give a description of a *free* life, especially if her duties are continually winning out in a conflict with her desires.

Questions of *freedom* of action aside, however, it is hard to see why Campbell's account should be thought adequate — or even relevant — as an account of substitutability, i.e., of claims that someone could have done otherwise than he did. Since, on his account, such claims are not justified when an agent acts on his strongest desire, their justification — a presupposition of obligability — requires that the motive of duty be *toto caelo* different from all other motives, which appear to be lumped under the head of *desire*. Allowing this point for the sake of the argument, we seem to confront a complete mystery when we face a 'conflict' between strongest desire and duty. Desire appears at the end of a natural chain of causes; duty appears — how? Certainly, as Campbell acknowledges, not by pure chance. There is, moreover, not just the question of the existence of the two sorts of motive, there is the question of their relative strengths. Again, on Campbell's account, the strength of the desire is set by natural forces outside our control; presumably the strength of our motivation to do our duty must be within our control, perhaps like the volume control of a radio which we can turn up until it drowns out the noisy (noisome?) cries of desire. Ignoring the picture, we still seem confronted with an obvious regress: we must, it seems, if we are voluntarily to control the strength of the motivation to do our duty, be *motivated* to control it. And so on. There seems no way out here. In any case, it appears obvious that whether or not — and to what extent — one is motivated by considerations of duty is not less a function of one's training than is whether or not — and to what extent — one is motivated by (any other) desire.

In addition to providing a dubious account of substitutability, Campbell's account of freedom provides what I take to be an obviously inadequate account of the scope of moral responsibility or obligability. Campbell's denial of the substitutability of actions performed on the basis of desires, together with his acceptance of the OES Supposition, yields his conclusion that such actions are not obligable. Now according to Campbell,

such a delimitation of the field of effective free will denies to the Libertarian absolutely nothing which matters to him. For it is precisely that small sector of the field of choices which our principle of delimitation still leaves open to free will — the sector in which strongest desire clashes with duty — that is crucial for moral responsibility. It is, I believe, with respect to such situations, and in the last resort to such situations alone, that the agent himself recognizes that moral praise and blame are appropriate. They are appropriate, according as he does or does not 'rise to duty' in the face of opposing desires ... .[14]

It seems clear to me that this statement far too narrowly limits the scope of moral responsibility, and, moreover, that it draws the distinction between the morally praiseworthy and the morally blameworthy at a dubious place. The first point can be dealt with quickly; there are all sorts of cases, both of praiseworthy actions and of blameworthy ones, into which the *clash* of duty and strongest desire simply does not enter. Suppose, e.g., that a person, simply out of a desire to help another person, saves that other person's life at the risk of his own. Surely an action so described would be praiseworthy, even though consideration of the agent's duty or obligation did not enter into the case, and, moreover, the clash Campbell speaks of did not occur, because thought of what he *ought* to do never crossed the agent's mind. In general, acts done under motives vaguely called *benevolent* appear as good candidates for praiseworthiness as do those under the motive vaguely labeled *duty*. Moreover, since an important part of the point of moral training is to give one the inclination to benevolent — as opposed to selfish — actions, to the extent that such training is successful to that extent one becomes incapable of what Campbell considers praiseworthy actions. Worse for Campbell's account is that since obligability extends only to cases of conflict between duty and desire, one can avoid blame-worthiness for even the most heinous crime simply by truly pleading that he paid no heed to consideration of what he ought to do! Thus, on Campbell's account, what would normally be considered an *in*culpating factor serves to exculpate. (I ignore, of course, the role of such a plea as part of a legal defense of insanity.)

Not only, however, does it seem clearly wrong to suppose that all cases of obligability necessarily involve a conflict of duty and desire, it appears that even in cases involving such a conflict, praiseworthiness need not characterize the triumph of duty, nor blameworthiness that of desire. Before arguing this point, let me make two points about the use of 'duty'. The first point, which may appear to be merely a verbal one, is that the notion of one's duty is not the same as, or coextensive with, the notion of what one ought to do. (The same point can be made about the notion of one's *obligation*, which like that of one's *duty*, is sometimes used as equivalent to that which one ought categorically to do.) If 'duty' is to have any special function — and it seems useful that it should — then it should be used to denote that which one is bound to do in virtue of some role or position which one holds; e.g. one's duties as soldier, teacher, parent, or whatever. On this conception of duty, a serious question may arise as to whether one ought on a given occasion to do what is unquestionably his duty (as say, a soldier). More importantly for our present purposes, if 'duty' denotes that which may be in psychological conflict with desire so that the resolution of the conflict is in any sense up to the agent, it must refer not to that which the agent abstractly ought to do, but to that which the agent believes or thinks that he ought to do. (And a defender of Campbell's position must guard against misuse of this possible ambiguity in the position.)

With these preliminaries out of the way, I want to suggest that the claims that an action is praiseworthy if (and only if) it involves the triumph of Apparent Ought (what one believes one ought to do) over Desire (what one wants to do, apart from those considerations which go into the Apparent Ought), and that an action is blameworthy if and only if it involves the triumph of Desire over Apparent Ought, are generalizations which, while having support in many cases, are subject to obvious counter-examples.

Consider, for example, the case of a soldier who, under orders, shoots innocent civilians. Surely the facts that the soldier had to overcome his natural revulsion in order to 'rise' to his duty and believed that he *ought* to obey his orders, do not render his action *praiseworthy*. Nor do they necessarily exculpate him – one need not hold with Aristotle that ignorance of the moral law is *never* an excuse, to recognize that such ignorance is often culpable, as *presumably* it would be in the case in question. Still, difficult questions of the justifiability of moral blame – as opposed, perhaps, to the justifiability of legal punishment – may remain in such a case. So it may be useful to mention a case in which the trappings of legitimacy are clearly absent. It is the case of a different sort of 'soldier', a member of a criminal organization, who is ordered to kill his brother because the latter has given information about the gang to the police. The order is given, of course, to test our hero's loyalty, since his extreme love for his brother is well known. Our hero, whose whole conception of a categorical imperative is bound up with his notion of loyalty to the group, overcomes, by a remarkable effort of will, all considerations of fraternal love, and does his 'duty'. Assuming that there are no other relevant facts in the case, 'blameworthy' would fail to apply only because it is too mild an epithet for such an horrendous act.

Surely, moreover, there is something odd about a theory which implies, e.g., that if newlyweds have sexual intercourse out of a sense of duty (it is demanded of them in their roles of husband and wife) or of obligation (it is a requirement of the marriage contract), then their actions are more praiseworthy than if performed out of – shall we say – inclination! But I have said enough, I believe, to indicate that Campbell's account limits obligability unduly, and, moreover, prescribes dubious moral judgments in those cases to which on its own terms it applies.

The excessive limitation on the application of the concept of obligability arises, as we saw, from Campbell's attempt to deal with the large degree of intelligibility and of predictability in the field of human behavior: most behavior he places in the realm of causal determination, and, hence, outside the realm of obligability. On his account such behavior is the result of desires, and is a manifestation of the agent's *character* (as opposed to the *self* which – or who? – is the author of those acts of which duty, not desire, is the prime mover; those acts are free and obligable). Now whether or not an agent's desires are to be accounted *causes* of his actions, in those cases, e.g., when they render the actions intelligible or predictable, is a question which I shall postpone until the next chapter. As we have seen, this is a point on which Campbell does appear to have been persuaded by determinists.

But if the explicability or the predictability of an agent's behavior, or of his characteristic behavior, is sufficient to show that it is subject to causation and hence (!) not obligable, then the distinction between obligable and non-obligable actions fails completely. For we can frequently *explain* human actions on the basis of agents' being motivated by a sense of duty or of moral obligation – frequently, i.e., relative to the number of occasions on which such motivation is operative. And, as with any other forms of motivation, the better we know individual persons, the better we can *predict* those cases in which they will act on such motivation, and, in particular, when they will act on such motivation in the face of temptation to do otherwise. Campbell may speak of cases of 'rising to one's duty' as manifestations of one's *self* rather than of one's *character*, but clearly a tendency to be motivated (more or less generally, more or less strongly) by considerations of what one ought to do can be as much a trait of *character* as the tendency to be motivated by considerations of pleasure. If predictability/explicability provides the criterion of causal determination, then it appears that Campbell has drawn his line at the wrong place. Explicability and, especially, predictability present obvious difficulties for cases on both sides of the line which Campbell has drawn; there seems little reason to suppose that inexplicability or unpredictability affects one class more than another in any significant way. In any event inexplicability of actions would appear tied more closely to notions like 'pure chance', "insanity", and other notions indicative of the absence of obligability than to the notion of freedom which is associated with its presence.

Campbell's account, then, may be seen as epitomizing, rather than as resolving, the problem of obligability. To the extent that an action is rendered intelligible by being subsumed under causal conditions, to that extent it is confronted by the determinist horn of the dilemma; to the extent it is not so explicable, to that extent it is confronted by the indeterminist horn. One final point should be made regarding this second alternative. On Campbell's account, it is not strictly speaking, the ('free') action which is inexplicable, for if we suppose that what Campbell calls 'duty' is a motivational factor, then the presence of that factor explains the occurrence of the action, just as in the case of other actions the presence of 'strongest desire' explains their occurrence. But here is where the problem becomes clear: if explicability of an action in terms of strongest desire renders it non-obligable because this desire is simply one element in an (indefinitely long) causal chain, then how are we better off so far as obligability is concerned when the occurrence of action is explicable in terms of the motivation of 'duty'? For it appears either that this motivation, like the others just mentioned, is itself a component in a causal sequence, or else the motivation, at, of course, a suitable level of strength, is just something the agent finds himself in possession of (or lacking). And of course, neither alternative puts the essential motivational condition in the control of the agent.

One last tug on the bootstrap: since the dilemma of obligability arises from treating as exhaustive the possibilities (a) that an action and its necessary causal conditions occur as components in an indefinitely long causal sequence, and (b) that the action and its causal conditions just inexplicably occur, perhaps we can suggest as a third possibility that the action is an element of a causal chain originating in the agent or self. Thereby the self would control the action and its causal antecedents, and hence assure the self's obligability. Such a view was suggested, and effectively criticized by Broad,[15] who stated that it is the view that "people who profess to belief in Free Will want to believe". More recently such eminent philosophers as Roderick Chisholm[16] and Richard Taylor[17] have attempted to reintroduce this view, on which the cause of an action is ultimately not another event in or disposition of the agent, but is rather a substance, namely the agent himself. Now this view does have the virtue of emphasiz-ing that the minimum unit of obligability is the individual agent,[18] and, perhaps, providing us with a reminder of the fact that it is our general practice, in assessing obligability, to trace back a series of causes until we come to (the action of) an agent.[19] But the view has some obvious difficulties.

Broad, indeed, claimed that it involved a view which is 'im-possible', the view, namely, that a substance can be the causal determinant of an event. (This is the essence of the view which Broad calls 'non-occurrent causation of events' and which Chisholm calls 'immanent' — as opposed to 'transeunt' — causation.) Broad writes:

I see no *prima facie* objection to there being events that are not completely determined. But, in so far as an event *is* determined, an essential feature in its total cause must be other *events*. How could an event possibly be deter-mined to happen at a certain date if its total cause contained no factor to which the notion of date has any application? And how can the notion of date have any application to anything that is not an event?[20]

Whether or not Broad's argument shows that notion of immanent causation to be impossible, it certainly shows it at least to be in need of a great deal of clarification. Contrary to what is implied in Broad's last (rhetorical) question, it does seem to make good sense to talk of the dates of a substance, and in particular, to refer to 'temporal slices' of an individual, although the *dating*, of course, is done *via* events. To be sure, to speak of an individual's dates is to speak of the dates between which the individual began and ceased to exist and to speak of X's existing is perhaps to speak of something event-like. But to speak of a temporal slice of an individual, i.e., considering substance during the interval t_1 to t_2, *is* to speak of a substance, not of an event. Still, this is of no help with the problem of assessing obligability, which, of course, is done with respect to agents, and not with respect to those temporal slices of agents which are contemporaneous with actions!

The difficulty connected with immanent causation which is suggested by Broad's statement is this: if there is no change of state in the agent (a dateable event) which is the determinant of his action, what (intelligible) is meant by the claim that *the agent caused* it? Chisholm sets himself this question, and answers:

The only answer, I think, can be this: that the difference between the man's causing *A*, on the one hand, and the event *A* just happening, on the other, lies in the fact that in the first case but not the second, the event *A was* caused and was caused by the man.[21]

"This answer", he adds, "may not entirely satisfy . . .", but he adds that we face here a difficulty in the very notion of causation: in no case of alleged causal connection *transeunt* or *immanent* can we say exactly what distinguishes the *post hoc* from the *propter hoc*, the case of *A*'s occurring being followed by *B*'s happening from the cases of *A*'s occurring being the *cause* of *B*'s occurring. Now, of course, Chisholm is quite familiar with all the talk of 'regularity of sequences' or 'lawlike connections' which are said to obtain in the case of causal relations, and to distinguish such relations from merely accidental sequences. Presumably, he judges that the difficulties in the definition of, say, 'law-like' are such as to render the use of such a term in the attempted clarification of the notion of cause unsatisfactory. Given the fact that in any discourse there must be unexamined notions, this represents a high standard of what constitutes clarity! But waiving the question of whether or not we can give a clear (enough?) account of transeunt causation, we can certainly recognize cases of it, as we can, it may be claimed, of immanent causation. But here is a significant difference: in cases of transeunt causation, we can use our knowledge to explain the particular events which occur as effects; often, moreover, we can predict and even control these effects. In cases of knowledge of immanent causation we can do none of these things: at best we can know that an agent performed a particular action, but to explain his performing that action rather than another we should have to appeal to something more — in fact, as Broad claims — to an event. Thus, if to state the cause of some event is to explain it — and this feature has been constantly attributed to causation since, at least Aristotle — or if to state the cause of some event is to state a sufficient condition for its occurrence, then the idea of immanent causation is indeed 'impossible'. In any case, since obligability for an action involves more than having done it (more, i.e., than *responsibility* in a weak sense) — it involves at least having done it in the absence of absolving conditions (i.e. conditions which remove one from considerations of praise or blame) — and since it is only conditions which serve to *explain* a particular action (e.g., that it was done under threat of death) which serve, e.g. to exculpate, the notion of immanent causation in failing to explain particular actions, fails to perform the function for which it was introduced — that of accounting for obligability.

It seems to me that the fundamental difficulty with the view that the notion of immanent causation can provide — and is needed to provide — a resolution to the dilemma of obligability lies — as does the basic difficulty with other views that maintain the OES supposition — in the OES supposition itself. Chisholm takes that supposition to imply a certain claim about responsibility or obligability, namely that if the act which a person

did perform was an act that was also in his power *not* to perform then *it* could not have been caused or determined by any event that was not itself within his power either to bring about or not to bring about . . . . if what we say he did was really something that was brought about by his own beliefs and desires . . . then, since *they* caused it, *he* was unable to do anything other than just what he did do. It makes no difference whether the cause of the deed was internal or external: if the cause was some state or event for which the man himself was not responsible, then he was not responsible for what we have been mistakenly calling his act.[22]

Now whether or not beliefs and desires are to be accounted *causes* of actions is a point which, I shall suggest, in the next chapter, has in the context of the free will controversy, been given undue prominence. Surely, however, we can often explain a person's action in a given situation on the basis of his desires or beliefs, and these may be said to determine him to act in a particular way. And, unless we are unduly influenced by some *a priori* theory, we are unlikely to suppose that we were mistaken in considering a deed an action, or in attributing it to an agent, on learning that the deed was brought about by the agent's desire. In any case, I shall argue in the next chapter that even with respect to those actions which epitomize the concept of human freedom there are sufficient conditions for their occurrence which are outside the control of the agent. The requirement that there not be such conditions is an impossible one, and if the OES supposition is interpreted as implying that requirement, the supposition is untenable.

A suggestion as to why this requirement is impossible may be obtained by looking at the end of the quotation from Chisholm, which embodies the requirement: "if the cause was some state or event for which the man himself was not responsible, then he was not responsible for .. ; his act". Now the appeal to causation of actions by the *self* is designed specifically to deal with this constraint, but complaints that such an appeal is *ad hoc* or unintelligible aside, it will not work. Since the appeal involves causation by *self*, it *a fortiori* sanctions the notion of immanent causation, i.e. causation by substances (including agents) rather than by events. But if we allow immanent causation, then clearly the restriction in the quoted requirement to 'some *state* or *event*' is indefensible. Surely, the point of the requirement is that an agent be not responsible for his action (or 'action' – the discovery of *some* kinds of causes does lead us to withdraw that particular description), if he is not responsible for its cause, of whatever category. Thus, if another agent is ultimately the (immanent) cause of our action (here, most likely 'action') then we may be absolved of obligability with respect to that action. Clearly, the requirement must be taken to be (roughly) "If a person is not responsible for the cause of his act, then he is not responsible for the act". Now a minimum condition of responsibility in the sense of the term here in question is that one be the causal agent of that for which he is responsible. But if the agent is the cause of his actions and is responsible for them only if he is the cause of *their* causes, then an agent is responsible for his actions only if he is the cause of himself. And this is absurd.

Moreover, if we think of immanent causation as causation by a *substance*, we must remember that we speak here of *substances* only in contrast to events or properties, and not as 'bare' particulars. I.e., in speaking of a particular *self* as cause, we should be referring to a flesh and blood agent with beliefs, desires, strengths, weaknesses, a certain height, weight, etc. And in saying this agent did something, we are surely not denying that if certain of these features had been different, he might (or would) have acted differently. Surely, then, in attributing obligability to the agent for the action, we must on the usual interpretation of the OES supposition attribute to him also responsibility for these relevant features, which are states of or events in the agent, and not themselves substances. But this brings us back to Broad's point, the impossibility of immanent causation's providing a complete account of the causation of human action.

In the next chapter we shall deal with an attempt to bypass the whole question of the causation of action which may now seem to be at the basis of the dilemma of obligability: if we trace back the chain of causes of an action, we must ultimately reach a link which is outside the causal control of the agent since clearly not caused by him, namely, either an event which occurred before his birth, an uncaused event, or the agent himself. Thus it is surely tempting to seek a way out of our dilemma which involves a rejection of the causal analysis of actions.

CHAPTER V

THE FLY IN THE FLYPAPER

In a famous image, Wittgenstein expressed his aim in philosophy as being that of showing 'the fly the way out of the fly-bottle'.[1] Surely, clearing up philosophical perplexity is one important philosophical task, one, indeed, which is a major part of my concern with the free will problem. Now the process of clarification may, for some philosophical puzzles, be adequately represented by Wittgenstein's image, but I suggest the image of the fly in the flypaper to depict an aspect of certain (sticky!) puzzles such as that of the one with which we are now dealing. The aspect to which I wish to call attention is suggested by the picture of the fly who can free a given leg from the flypaper, but only by entangling another one (or more). In this chapter I want to suggest that as long as we maintain the OES supposition our puzzle will remain a sticky one: that we will overcome one difficulty only at the expense of being entangled in another.

We have just noted the difficulties involved if we construe human actions as among those events to which the notion of causality is applicable: either we trace back the causal sequence incorporating the action to events, or states, occurring prior to the agent's birth, or we trace them back to uncaused events or states. In either, the action has causal antecedents over which the agent has no control, and this fact gives rise to the question of the agent's obligability. We have looked at one attempt to deal with this dilemma — by an appeal to the notion of immanent causation. Let us now consider the suggestion that human actions are to be accounted neither events in a long causal chain, nor random and inexplicable events, on the ground that the notion of causality cannot intelligibly be applied to them. It seems to me that the arguments for this last claim are unpersuasive, but, more importantly, that even if it be granted that human actions do not fall under the cause-effect rubric, still this admission, far from resolving the dilemma of obligability, leads to a clear demonstration that the dilemma can be resolved only by eliminating the OES supposition.

The view that human actions are neither merely chance events nor parts of a causal chain rests on an analysis of these actions on which they are to be explained in terms of the agent's (motivating) reasons for acting (notably certain of his beliefs or desires) — and hence are not random events — but in terms of which the action is not *caused*, since the agent's reasons are not *causes* of the action.[2] It is this last point which has stirred up the greatest controversy,[3] and we shall look at the argument for it shortly.

If indeterminism is simply the denial of determinism, then the view now being considered, which I shall call 'action analysis', is a form of indeterminism. But it is important to distinguish action analysis from other forms of indeterminism, e.g., that of Campbell, in terms of which many, if not most, human actions are *causally* explicable in terms of the agent's desires. Even if an indeterminist were to claim that no actions have *causes*, if this claim were intended as one of contingent fact and not of conceptual necessity, it would differ in this essential respect from that of the action analyst.

Action analysis is closely tied to a view of language in terms of which it is compartmentalized in certain ways. This Kiplingesque ('never the twain shall meet') view appears manifested in *one* use which Wittgensteinians give to the term 'language-game', namely, to refer to a segment of language which involves a set of interrelated concepts, and which is conceptually separate from the rest of the language. (The suggestion is that illegitimate questions arise from the attempt to violate this logical apartheid.)

Action analysis makes a sharp distinction between human actions and bodily movements, between, e.g., one's raising one's arm, and one's arm going up, and assigns these concepts to different language games. The language game of actions involves such concepts as reason and responsibility — but not cause (which *is* involved in the language game of bodily movements). Thus this last notion simply has no possible application to human actions, much as, say, the notion of a home run would apply to nothing in the game of football. But the correctness of this analysis hardly stares us in the face; surely, as far as ordinary use goes, we frequently hear and seemingly understand talk of actions being caused (e.g., "John's fear of flying caused him to take the train", or "Connie's desire to help her husband's career caused her to neglect her own opportunities for education"), and so we need some argument designed to show that at least in some important sense of 'cause', the term does not apply to human action.

Action analysts have developed an argument for the claim that the agent's motivating reasons, which are the obvious candidates for the role of causes of actions, cannot properly be so accounted. The argument is based on the claim that a cause and its effect must be logically distinct from each other, while a reason, e.g. a desire to perform a certain action, is logically related to the action. The doctrine that a cause must be logically distinct from its effect is attributed to Hume.[4] One may well wonder whether Hume conceived as *logical* any relation other than entailment and concepts interdefinable with it. (And surely no one maintains that [a statement of] the occurrence of a desire *entails* [a statement of] the occurrence of the desired action.) Even, however, if Hume *did* conceive of a logical relation weaker than entailment, unless we are prepared to accept Hume's account of causation as in all respects authoritative, we may still hesitate to accept the doctrine under consideration. We can, of course, *stipulate* that nothing is to count as a cause which is not — in a sense not yet specified — 'logically independent' of its effect, but obviously such stipulation cannot resolve any substantive question as to the relations which in fact obtain between what are standardly recognized as cause and effect.

The action analyst's argument proceeds with the claim — or stipulation — that logically independent events must be capable of independent description, i.e., that if two events are logically independent, then it must be possible to give a specification of one which does not involve a reference to the other. Now one would suppose that the logical independence of events would require only the possibility of their independent *occurrence* — a feature which clearly characterizes desires to act and actions, since one neither desires to do everything he does, nor does everything he desires to do. That logically independent events must be independently describable may, however, be construed as part of the action analyst's conception of *logical independence*, although on this construction the claim that causes and effects *must be* logically independent is hardly self-evident.

In any event, the argument concludes that a desire to act cannot be the cause of the resulting action, since the two components are not logically independent: a description of the desire necessarily makes reference to the action desired. This last point is by no means obviously true. Desires might be singled out, e.g., by reference to the time of their inception, or, more speculatively, by reference to their related brain states. To be sure, explanation in terms of desires so described would be lacking in perspicuity, but so, as Hume was well aware, are explanations in terms of (Humean) causal relations based on contiguity and constant conjunction. Parenthetically, the inadequacy of Hume's account of causality — on which, as we have seen, the doctrine now under discussion is expressly based — is perhaps nowhere more clearly seen than in the central Humean doctrine that every idea is derived from an antecedent impression. This derivation can be nothing but *causal*, but obviously there is no constant conjunction between impressions and ideas – the latter would have little function if there were – and the very applicability of the notion of contiguity to this kind of case is questionable.

In any event, an explanation of an action in terms of a desire is not paradigmatically exemplified by statements of the form '*X* did *A* because *X* wanted to do *A*'. When we consider actual cases of explanations of actions in terms of desires we find that although the desires in question *are* normally specified by reference to their objects, these objects are rarely just the actions to be explained. More commonly they are states of affairs to which the actions to be explained stand in a means-ends, or perhaps part-whole, relation, or else they involve alternative descriptions of the actions in question. Hence, if it is claimed that the explanation of an action in terms of a desire requires that the specification of the desire makes a reference to the action, this reference is usually at most indirect, and is required, if at all, only on some presupposed model of 'complete explanation'. When, for example, I say that I am swallowing aspirin because I want to be rid of a headache, the description of my desire makes no direct reference to my action.

Another sort of example should serve to show the doubtful validity of the demand for the independent describability of cause and effect. Suppose that I discover that whenever I utter a statement of the form 'I wish that *X* were dead' the individual named dies – apparently of natural causes – immediately afterwards. Experimenting in a detached scientific manner, I find that my use of the utterance in question is invariably 'successful'. Surely, after a time I should be justified in concluding that (in some mysterious way) my utterances were causing the deaths of the persons involved. I should henceforth have to be very careful – or at least very selective – in what I said. But in the action analyst's sense, the utterances and the deaths would not be logically independent because they would not be independently describable. It would seem, therefore, that the logical requirement of independent describability of causally related events is unwarranted. The same point can be made with respect to many other cases, ranging from such prosaic instances as giving a causal explanation of why a piece of ice is just such and such a shape to such esoteric examples as giving a causal explanation of the derivation of ideas from (independently described!) impressions.

The failure of this argument to show that reasons for actions cannot be causes does not, of course, demonstrate that they are, nor does it demonstrate that there is not some sort of 'conceptual connection' between reasons and actions. But I want to maintain that neither of these questions is of great moment as far as the resolution of our dilemma goes. Indeed, the question of whether reasons are causes threatens to dissolve into a merely verbal issue: on the one hand, the terms 'reason' and 'cause' do not have precisely determined ranges of application, and in many contexts they are virtually interchangeable; moreover, reasons (an agent's pro-attitudes and beliefs) serve a similar explanatory function with respect to human actions to that performed by (other) causes with respect to *their* effects. On the other hand, reasons can be distinguished from (other) causes — as the possibility of raising the question of their relationship is sufficient to show — in virtue of features of justification and intensionality. (The statement of *reasons* tends to provide a *justification* — at least in the eyes of the agent[5] — as well, thereby, as an explanation of an action; whether R is a *reason* for A depends in part on how R and A are described: neither of these features seems to characterize non-teleological causal explanations.) Whether, then, we are to say that reasons are a sub-class of causes — in virtue of their similarities — or that reasons constitute a distinct class from causes — in virtue of their differences — appears not to be a substantive question so long as we are straight about the facts.[6]

The distinction of reasons from (other) causes may, of course, be worth insisting on in certain contexts. It would be in the present context, e.g., if an action's being done for a reason were a reliable index of its being obligable; unfortunately, it appears not to be. Indeed, that an action is done for a reason would seem to be neither a necessary nor a sufficient condition of its being obligable. The most obvious case of an *action* which is done other than for a reason is one done out of habit. To give an explanation of an action in terms of habit is to give an explanation in terms of causes as opposed to reasons, in terms of etiology rather than in terms of teleology. But while habituation may *explain* our performing an action, it does not generally *absolve* us of responsibility for its performance — in case something turns on that in a particular instance — nor, e.g. does it absolve us of obligability for neglecting to perform some morally required alternative action. On the other hand even if an action is performed for a reason, it is not *ipso facto* obligable; indeed, the nature of the reason may be such that its occurrence may be just what constitutes an absolving condition. Faced e.g., with criminal threats, one may perform an action such as giving up a sum of money which is in one's keeping, out of a desire to save one's life, without necessarily doing something blameworthy (or praiseworthy). It is worth noting here that this sort of case is one of which it is typically said that the agent 'couldn't do otherwise', where this claim has the force of denying the agent's obligability rather than of describing the state of the agent's faculties or abilities.

If we agree that an action's being done for a reason is neither a necessary nor a sufficient condition of its being obligable, then we would appear to have less reason to concern ourselves with the question of whether reasons for actions are to be classified as causes. Still, if we recall that the dilemma of obligability has traditionally been set forth in terms of the language of causality we may understand a tendency to suppose that we might bypass the problem if we could show that the notion of causality is inapplicable to human actions — or at least to those actions which are paradigms of freedom. As will become obvious below, I do not want to deny that those actions which are paradigmatically free are those which are done for reasons, even though I have denied that being so done is a necessary condition of being free, at least insofar as this latter notion is tied to that of obligability. But even if we proclaim a strict separation between the language games of action and of bodily movement, and restrict the applicability of 'cause' (or of ' "cause" strictly speaking') to the latter, this legislative decree will fail, on two levels, to resolve the dilemma of obligability, and, indeed, will render it — given the OES supposition — more manifestly insoluble.

Assuming the logical apartheid of the concepts of human actions and bodily movements — and one may surely wonder whether a similar distinction applies in the case of animals other than human — and for the sake of argument restricting the application of 'cause' to bodily movements, still we find that when we raise the question of the causation of these movements, the Dilemma of Obligability arises in only a slightly altered form.[7]

Bodily movements may be characterized, adequately for present purposes, as motions of a (human) body, or of any of its parts, e.g., the change of position of Mary's body from one side of the room to the other, Henry's arm going up, John's lips parting, or Jessica's vocal cords vibrating. Clearly, most human actions involve bodily movements: Mary can't cross the room, e.g., without her body's moving from one side of the room to the other. The qualification 'most' is designed to deal with those cases which we account actions, e.g., refraining from voting, keeping silent, or standing motionless, which do not involve specific bodily movements (although they rule some out). It will simplify our discussion, without distorting it, if we omit consideration of such cases, and consider only those actions which essentially involve particular bodily movements.

The relationship between actions and bodily movements is obviously of central importance for our problem. It seems clear that, as the action analysts have insisted, actions are not to be characterized as bodily movements plus mental accompaniments ('acts of volition', or whatever). On this point it is perhaps sufficient to note that we can normally tell that an agent is doing (signing his name, playing a Beethoven sonata, opening a can of sardines) without having to inquire into his accompanying mental state. Difficulties in the view that actions are to be analyzed as bodily movements plus mental accompaniments are familiar,[8] and I shall not review them here.

Rejection of this view is thought to be of importance for action analysis, since if every action necessarily involved independently identifiable mental events, it might be claimed that these events are causes. But, one may wonder, causes of what? We saw above that the action analyst's conception of cause is such as to require the logical independence of cause and effect. Hence, the view which the action analyst is at such pains to reject, namely, that actions are bodily movements plus mental accompaniments, is no threat to his analysis: the putative mental accompaniment, being an essential component of the action cannot be a *cause* of the action − at least on the action analyst's use of 'cause'. And, as we have seen, he wants to maintain only that *actions* cannot significantly be said to have causes: he is more than willing to allow that the question of the causation of bodily movements is a significant one.

But if bodily movements have causes − or even if they do not! − then, given the relationship between these movements and actions, namely, that under suitable circumstances a bodily movement *is* an action; we are confronted anew with the Dilemma of Obligability. Elimination of reference to accompanying mental states from the analysis of the concept of action removes one source of obfuscation − and anyone dissatisfied with this elimination may simply think of the mental accompnaiments as components of the 'suitable circumstances', which, in any event, are extremely complex, mentioned in the preceding sentence. But now, given the OES supposition, a clear difficulty confronts us. Consider any bodily movement M. Either M is an element in a causal chain which goes back indefinitely, or else M itself or one of its causal antecedents is a purely chance event. (The *tertium quid* which allegedly applies to *actions* clearly has no application in the totally separate language game of bodily movements.) But in neither case can M be reasonably claimed to be under the control of any agent. Suppose now that M occurs under circumstances such that M constitutes an action. Since M is either a random event or else the causal consequent of events over which no agent has present control, it might appear unreasonable to hold the individual whose bodily movement M is, accountable for M, or, consequently, for the action which is under the circumstances identical with M.

The foregoing dilemma is set forth solely to argue for the point that the Dilemma of Obligability is not to be resolved by the action analyst's distinction of actions and bodily movements, with the category of causation being applicable only to members of the latter class. It is *not* employed to show that human beings are — or must be — deterministic or non-deterministic automata, although the sharp separation of bodily movements from actions may tend, if we focus on the former, to give rise to such a picture. Nor, surely, is our argument designed to obscure the obvious fact that human beings are capable of initiating actions. Anyone needing reassurance on this point need merely start to twiddle his thumbs (if he is not already doing so).

If concentration on the cause-bodily movement language game forcefully suggests that the distinction of reasons from causes provides no solution to the Dilemma of Obligability, this suggestion is strongly reinforced by attention to the language game of reasons and actions. The denial that actions have causes can give only the wrong kind of reassurance with respect to our Dilemma, the false sense of security gotten, e.g., by the man who moves to a Pacific island and is assured that there is no danger of hurricanes in his new location. (He later discovers that the windstorm which has destroyed his home is here called a typhoon.) For there are sufficient conditions of actions – whether or not these conditions are accounted causes – and these conditions are not *up to* the agent even when the action itself is – and is freely performed.

Consider abstractly some action A. This consideration, incidentally, while abstract, will be no more so than has been the traditional treatment of the component claims of the Dilemma of Obligability, notably including that of the supposition that 'ought' implies 'can' (what I have been calling the OES supposition). Now if A is to be a paradigm of a free action, it cannot be performed against the agent's will; we can fairly assume that at the time the agent performed A there was no other action he would have preferred to perform. Also, if A is to be paradigmatically free, its agent must not have been lacking relevant knowledge which, at the time he decided to do A, he might reasonably have been expected to possess. The foregoing may be thought of as factors in the absence of which an action would not have been totally free; there is no suggestion that these factors provide either a sufficient basis for an action's being free, or a necessary condition of an action's being obligable. The question of the possible culpability of the agent's ignorance may cast doubt on the latter point, while the question of the etiology of the agent's desire may serve to undermine the former. (No one, I suppose, would suggest that the language games of 'reason' and of 'cause' are *so* disparate that we may not intelligibly speak of causes of desires. In any event, if, say, an agent's strongest desire at the time he pays a ransom is to save his child's life, and the pre-eminence of this desire results from a kidnaper's threat to kill that child, then the action of paying the ransom is hardly one which would qualify as an examplar of the notion of a free action.)

In addition to these factors of pre-eminent desire and of adequate knowledge, there are other general conditions which, being necessary conditions of any action are *a fortiori* necessary conditions of any free action. These factors may be denominated — again speaking very abstractly — those of ability and of opportunity. Both of these terms are intended to apply very broadly; thus, 'ability' includes reference to such notions as skill, strength, endurance and 'know-how', while 'having the opportunity to perform an action' incorporates such notions as having suitable means, instruments, equipment, etc., as well as having a suitable location and (social or other) position. (The notions of ability and opportunity obviously overlap a great deal, and we could, if we liked, consider the latter a sub-class of the former.)

Let us now suppose that at some time t, an agent has a pre-eminent desire to do A (i.e., desires to perform A and desires to perform no action more than he desires to perform A), has the requisite relevant knowledge with respect to A (including, e.g., knowledge of the probable consequences of A, of the nature of the available alternatives to A and of their consequences, of his ability to do A, and of how to do A), and, moreover, has (at t) the ability and the opportunity to do A. It seems clear that these conditions are sufficient for the agent's doing A. But it also seems obvious that whether or not these conditions obtain at time t is not up to the agent at t, at least in the way in which the action A is thought to be up to its agent at t. Now the resolution of the Dilemma of Obligability turns on the recognition that there is nothing paradoxical — and surely nothing self-contradictory — about there being actions which are up to an agent even though these actions have sufficient conditions which are *not* similarly up to this agent — and, moreover, (a somewhat different point) that the agent may be obligable for such actions.

That an agent may be obligable with respect to an action whose performance or non-performance is not at the time of its performance (or non-performance) up to the agent is a claim that I shall develop more fully in the next chapter.

Here is may be useful to recall that determinism is alleged to be worrisome because if it is true "there will be for any action a set of sufficient conditions which can be traced back to factors outside the control of the agent".[9] If this description of an action is worrisome − as ruling out the possibility of 'substitutability' − then we have even a good deal more to worry about than we normally suppose. As we have seen, if determinism is false, so that the sufficient conditions of actions can be traced back to uncaused events, then this description applies, in that uncaused or purely chance events are clearly 'outside the control of the agent'. What I am maintaining now is that if, for the sake of argument, we waive the question of whether or not an agent's reasons for acting are *causes* of his action, that there are sufficient conditions of even actions which are paradigmatically free − whether or not all these conditions are denominated *causal* − which conditions are not up to or within the control of the agent. Hence, on the account in question, we shall have to be seriously worried about those actions which are most clearly free and up to their agents, and *a fortiori* about all actions. This strongly suggests that we should be less concerned about the actions described in the account − which appears to include *all* actions − and more worried about the account itself.

Consider once again our schematic account: at some time t, an agent has the ability, the opportunity, the awareness of this ability and this opportunity, and the desire to do A. He has, moreover, no stronger (conflicting) desire at t. Under the conditions described, the agent does A: the conditions are sufficient for his doing A. It may be said that these conditions are *trivially* sufficient, that, e.g., if an agent has the ability and the opportunity to do A, and the awareness of these, but does not do A, then this is sufficient to show that doing A is not what he is most strongly motivated to do. The principal point to note with regard to this observation is that it does not constitute an *objection* to our procedure; for present purposes it need only be *true* that the conditions specified are sufficient for the action A; it need not be non-trivially true. To be sure, if the account were designed as a schema for the explanation (or prediction) of A, it would be obviously inadequate, primarily because no independent criterion − independent, i.e., of the performance of the action − is provided for the determination that the motive operative at t is the agent's *strongest*. We may note, incidentally, that the notion of *strongest desire* is presupposed in our everyday explanations of behavior in terms of motives. (The presence of a desire normally leading to the doing of A would not explain the agent's doing A if he had a stronger conflicting desire.) If the sort of account provided by our schema is inadequate as an *explanation* of actions it is so because the sufficient conditions are too closely (logically, conceptually) tied to the action accounted for. The task of *explanation* then becomes that of providing an explanation (ultimately, one supposes, causal) of these sufficient conditions. But surely one doesn't show that an agent 'could have done otherwise' by showing that his action was not *causally* necessitated by conditions obtaining but (merely!) *logically* necessitated by these conditions.

Let us suppose, then, that we have specified (schematized and trivial) sufficient conditions for an action A. If, incidentally, I have overlooked some sort of consideration(s) which must hold at t in order for the conditions specified to be sufficient, let the reader be generous enough to supply it (them): my argument will not thereby be affected. Non-trivial questions − non-trivial, i.e., from the point of view of one concerned with the Dilemma of Obligability − are then (a) are these conditions up to the agent?

(b) can they be traced back to factors outside the control of the agent? and (c) what, if anything, is the relevance of our answers to these questions to be the further questions as to whether A is up to its agent and whether A is obligable? It seems to me that the OES supposition, as operative within the Dilemma of Obligability, involves the twin claims that if an action is to be up to an agent, the sufficient conditions of that action must not be traceable to factors outside the control of the agent, and that if an action is to be accounted obligable it must be up to its agent. Hence, that an action is not obligable if there are sufficient conditions for the action which can be traced back to factors outside the agent's control. In the remainder of this chapter I want to argue that on this reading the OES supposition sets a standard of obligability which no action can meet. In the next chapter, I want to discuss the nature of the OES supposition further and to argue that it, rather than the notion of obligability, is what is suspect.

My argument can be made in terms of the questions formulated above. The answer to the first question, as to whether the conditions of A are up to the agent must, as we shall see, be equivocal, although, I shall maintain, these conditions are not up to the agent in the way that a free action is. This last point can perhaps be made clear in terms of the notion of a command: an action, disposition, or psychological set may be thought of as up to an individual ('subject to his will') at a given time if at that time he can perform or adopt it on command.[10] Now while action A in our schema may be supposed to be such an action, i.e., while we may readily suppose A to be an action which can be done on command, it normally makes no sense even to command someone (here and now) to have the ability or the desire to do A. One must not suppose, of course, that if an action is up to an agent its necessary conditions are similarly up to the agent (having been born, e.g., is only one of an indefinitely large number of necessary conditions of any action which are hardly up to the agent): all that is required generally of necessary conditions of actions which are up to an agent is that they be satisfied, not that their satisfaction be up to the agent. This is obvious enough, but still it may be thought that if there are sufficient conditions of an action which are not up to an agent the action *ipso facto* cannot be up to the agent. It may indeed be granted that having the desire, ability, and opportunity to do *A* may not generally be up to the agent as *A* is, i.e., capable of being present on command, but, still that if they − or some of them − weren't in some sense up to the agent, that if they were just there regardless of what the agent did or had done, then they could not be up to the agent. We do, of course, distinguish between those conditions of action which would − or might − have been different, had an agent earlier acted differently, from those conditions which would not have been so affected by the agent's actions, and even denominate the former sorts of conditions − in contrast to the latter − as being up to the agent.

Now if an avowed determinist were to make the point that on his doctrine, too, different actions on the part of agents would have been followed by different consequences, including different causal antecedents of actions, his opponent would surely raise the question of whether, granted the truth of the determinist's hypothetical claim, there was any possibility, on the deterministic view, of there being different actions performed by any agents. An analogous question ought surely to be raised with regard to the distinction now under consideration, namely, between those conditions of action which are up to an agent and those which are not − a distinction, incidentally, which may be of significance for the question of obligability, even if not, ultimately, for that of substitutability. Granted that we account conditions of action as up to the agent if prior actions of the agent would have altered those conditions (one's desires, abilities, or opportunities would

have been relevantly different had he acted differently earlier),
the question next arises with regard to these possible alternative
actions: since they did not occur, obviously their sufficient
conditions did not occur: was it up to the agent nonetheless
to bring them about? Well, it was up to him, if his having acted
differently earlier would have brought about those conditions.
And so on. Clearly, this sort of analysis provides no way out of
our Dilemma, since it leads in a finite number of steps to actions
and conditions of actions which, occurring in infancy or earlier,
are clearly not up to the agent. We have hereby answered our
second question: the sufficient conditions of even an action
normally accounted free *can be* traced back to factors outside
the control of the agent. But, I submit, (in answer to our third
question) the fact that sufficient conditions of action are not
up to the agent in the way that an action may be (occurring on
command, or at will), and, moreover, that these conditions can be
traced back to factors outside the control of the agent, are not
directly relevant even to the question of whether an action is up
to its agent, let alone to the question of whether it is an obligable
action.

It may be natural enough to suppose − or to require − that
if a proposed action is to be accounted (really) up to an agent or
(really) free, its sufficient conditions must similarly be up to the
agent. But this supposition, leading as it does to the 'tracing
back to factors' must ultimately lead us to some factors outside
the agent's control. Now we could conclude from this that no
action is really up to its agent (although without a further *a priori*
ruling, this would not decide the question of whether or not some
actions are obligable), or we could seriously consider distinctions
among particular possible cases (considering, e.g., cases of individuals who are paralyzed, shackled, drugged, hypnotized, terrified,
untrained, etc. in contrast with cases of individuals who are
not so limited, with respect to which actions are up to them),

with a view to questioning whether or not we have formulated an adequate criterion of what it is for an action to be up to an agent.

It seems to me that the resolution of the Dilemma of Obligability will not result from the determination we make concerning the question of whether the reasons for actions are demonstrated its *causes*. Rather it will come when we recognize that for an action to be obligable or even up to its agents it is not necessary for its sufficient conditions to be similarly up to the agent. The supposition that it is necessary — essentially what I have called the OES supposition — is what makes the resolution of this ancient puzzle impossible. By setting logically unattainable standards of obligability the OES supposition causes a self-induced puzzlement to masquerade as a problem.

CHAPTER VI

OUGHTS AND CANS

J. L. Austin opened his celebrated paper 'Ifs and Cans'[1] with the question, "Are *cans* constitutionally iffy?" Now, whatever answer one gives to this question, I want to maintain, against the tradition which holds that 'ought' implies 'can', that some *oughts* may be positively uncanny. Or rather, I want to argue that 'ought' does not entail 'can' (i.e., I want to argue against the OES supposition) – insofar as 'can' is used in such a way that the determinism/indeterminism question has a bearing on the claim that someone *can* act (or could have acted) otherwise than he will (or did). Thus, if to say that an agent could have acted otherwise is taken as implying that his action did not have sufficient conditions which were, or could be traced back to factors which were, outside the agent's control, then on this use of 'could' (or of 'can'), determinism/indeterminism is relevant to the question of substitutability. It seems clear that some such notion of substitutability – i.e., of '*X* could have done otherwise' – along, of course, with the OES supposition, underlies the Dilemma of Obligability. Since my concern is with this Dilemma, and especially with its untenable conclusion that the notion of obligability can have no application, my concern is with such a conception of substitutability which, as a component of the OES supposition, would support that conclusion. My further concern, obviously is to argue against the supposition.

An alternative strategy for combatting the unacceptable conclusion of the Dilemma of Obligability involves accepting the OES supposition, but construing substitutability in such a way that it is compatible with determinism or with indeterminism.

(preferably with both: it would be signally unfortunate to have the possibility of practical judgments dependent on such an abstruse — indeed untestable — metaphysical issue as the truth of determinism.) Such a construal, if it is to be of any interest, must be reasonably consonant with our ordinary ways of talking; it must not involve the arbitrary redefinition of terms which might, e.g., render 'all pigs fly' a truth, or even a necessary truth. Now, I have suggested above that in certain contexts to say that an agent could (not) have done otherwise is, in effect, to claim that he was (not) obligable for his action. One could conceivably — though not very plausibly — generalize from such cases to the *identification* of substitutability and obligability. Such an identification would trivially yield the OES supposition without adding new problems about determinism/indeterminism. But, of course, substitutability and obligability are not identical, and if they were, the lack of one could not be used to justify the lack of the other (the claim that one could not have done otherwise would not be a *ground* for the claim that he was not responsible for what he had done), unless it is thought that one justifies a claim by repeating it.

I mention the foregoing 'solution' to the problem posed by the Dilemma of Obligability only because I wish to suggest that apart from some such identification of substitutability and obligability or some move involving the redefinition of one or both of the terms ('substitutability' and 'obligability') it is hard to see how one could reasonably hope to sustain the claim that obligability *entails* substitutability. Generally those who support the claim appear to consider it too obvious to require argument. Broad, for example, in the article referred to above, says, "We all admit that there is some sense or other of 'could' in which 'ought' and 'ought not' entail 'could'".[2] And another equally careful philosopher, Roderick Chisholm, writes, "If a choice is one we could not have avoided making, then it is one for which we are not morally responsible". He comments that this premise 'may be interpreted as a logical truth', which is equivalent to the OES supposition, and then adds

If a man is responsible for what he did, then we may say, "He could have done otherwise." And if we may say, "He couldn't help it," then he is not responsible for what he did." [3]

Surely this addition is to be taken as at best an explication and not as a justification of the entailment claim.

To see the dubious nature of this claim, one may consider cases of a sort which best serve to support it. Suppose, for example, that a person fails to fulfill an obligation because an illness or injury befalls him which prevents him from doing so. And, to simplify the discussion, let us suppose further that the circumstances are such that we should, in fact, not account the agent responsible for failing to fulfill the obligation. (It was not the case, e.g., that the disabling disease or injury was due to the agent's deliberate action or to his carelessness.) Even here, in the most favorable sort of case, in which we suppose the circumstances to be such that it is true that the agent's inability to perform an action renders him non-obligable with respect to it, does this tend to support the claim that this is a *necessary* truth, that, in other words, non-substitutability *entails* non-obligability? That it does not can be seen, I believe, by considering the sort of mistake that would be made by a person – or group – who, recognizing the circumstances of the agent's inability to fulfill his obligation nonetheless wished to hold him responsible for not doing so; and by our recognizing – as the reference to the *circumstances* of the action should suggest – that the relationship between obligability and substitutability lacks the requisite generality to be one of entailment. One fact that should emerge from our discussion is one which is anyway perhaps obvious enough on a little reflection, namely, that assertions of obligability or of non-obligability are themselves practical (evaluative) judgments. It is perhaps suggestive, in this regard, that we use locutions such as 'holding persons responsible (obligable)'; we don't similarly '*hold* agents able to do otherwise' since we consider such questions of ability to be ones of fact quite independent of our judgments of them.

Be this as it may, what sort of mistake would be made by someone who, in a case in which an agent's inability absolved him of obligability, nonetheless insisted that it did not, and that, e.g., the agent ought to be punished for acting (or failing to act)? Obviously, if obligability *entailed* substitutability, the mistake involved would be purely logical or semantical; we should have a case of self-contradiction, and of the sort of challenge to intelligibility which confronts us when we are told, for example, that A is taller than B but that B is not shorter than A. Surely, the most plausible account of the mistake appeals not to the dissident's odd use of words or faulty logic (although this appeal is — trivially — always available in attempting to account for another's error) but rather to defects in his moral judgment or character. He may, e.g., have a faulty — excessively strict — view of certain moral precepts, believing that there is no excuse — ever — for lying or for breaking a promise. Or he may be excessively vindictive, or lacking in empathy or sympathy. In any event, for an individual — or a society — to have, with respect to certain classes of moral offenses excessively strict criteria of obligability — even including 'strict liability', i.e., criteria allowing for *no* excuses, may serve no useful function (it may fail, e.g., to reduce the number of such offenses); even if functional, the employment of such criteria may be uncompassionate and even cruel. But to say that it is pointless or unfair to blame or to punish a person for an action — even for one which he couldn't help performing — is to make a practical or moral judgment; it is far different to suggest that the description of the blaming or punishing is logically incoherent. To be sure, even this suggestion could be made by one who *defined* 'blame' or 'punishment' in such a way that he refused to apply these terms to certain ways of dealing with an agent for actions having certain characteristics (e.g. being, in some sense, unavoidable), but if these consequences were exactly like those which otherwise would be labeled 'blame' or 'punishment', then clearly the suggestion would be of no substantive interest, and could be circumvented by introducing alternative terminology.

Perhaps most proponents of the claim that 'ought' implies 'can' would admit without argument that their claim is a moral and not a logical one, being in effect the claim that one *ought* to be held responsible only for those actions which he is able to perform or to refrain from performing. What suggests that the claim is a logical one is, perhaps, the occurrence in it of 'implies'. This occurrence can be explained by the lack in English of a one word expression for 'is a sufficient condition of': 'implies' is at least, in some contexts, close to this meaning. Unfortunately, its use between quoted expressions does further suggest the notion of logical implication or entailment. Anyway, recognizing that 'ought' implies 'can' — which, for short, I shall continue to call the OES supposition — embodies a moral or practical claim, we must take a further look at it in connection with the Dilemma of Obligability. Note that unless the OES supposition did embody such a claim, the Dilemma would not present us with a *practical* problem at all: and moreover, that this supposition, if it embodies a true moral claim can function formally as well in the Dilemma as it could if it were construed as logically necessary. I.e., as long as the OES supposition is true, whether it be a truth of logic or of morality, it functions adequately as a premise of the Dilemma.

Near the beginning of 'Ifs and Cans',[4] Austin writes, "In philosophy, there are many mistakes that it is no disgrace to make: to make a first-water, ground-floor mistake, so far from being easy, takes one (*one*) form of philosophical genius". Well, surely sometimes this is so, but we must not be captivated by the picture of the slightly-mad genius. Many philosophical mistakes have their origins in features, such as what Wittgenstein called 'the craving for generality', which are far more widely distributed in the human population than is genius. Lying at the heart of the perplexity over free will and obligability is the OES supposition. This supposition, I wish to maintain, embodies a 'first-water, ground-floor mistake', but one which arises not out of genius, but rather out of an inaccurate generalization of the conditions which absolve agents of responsibility for their actions.

It ought to strike us as strange that generations of philosophers brought up on the doctrine of the logical apartheid of the 'normative' and the 'descriptive' (and perhaps even having serious qualms about the 'cognitive significance' of the former) should appear to subscribe unhesitatingly to the OES supposition.[5] Perhaps the denial of the supposition may suggest to some philosophers the odd-sounding doctrine that we may sometimes be required to do the impossible. This point needs looking into. But we should note that for a philosopher 'doing the impossible' typically suggests squaring circles or walking on water, and the question of our obligation to perform such feats hardly constitutes the central question of moral philosophy.

I have suggested that the OES supposition represents an inaccurate (over-) generalization of those conditions which do absolve an agent of obligability. We are taking the supposition as a practical or moral generalization: the test of its acceptability, as of any other such generalization's, must be in its coherence with our other practical principles and considered particular moral judgments. I shall return to this point below. But whatever the source of the initial plausibility of the OES supposition, and whatever its inadequacies as a moral generalization as shown by particular examples, its overall inadequacy as a formulation of a criterion of (non-)obligability is shown by the Dilemma of Obligability itself. With respect to that Dilemma, we may note first the paradoxical feature that a practical claim (the OES supposition) appears as a premise in an argument purporting to show that the notion of obligability has no application, and this is tantamount to the conclusion that there can be no practical claims. If, moreover, the OES supposition, as stating a criterion of obligability yields the conclusion that no actions are or can be obligable, we must surely question the supposition, and recognize the it clearly fails to capture our standard criterion of obligability and non-obligability. Rather than being a demonstration of the impossibility of obligable actions, the Dilemma may be viewed as a *reductio ad absurdum* of the OES supposition. It might be thought that we have a simple standoff, with the OES supposition implying the impossibility of obligability, and with the apparent fact of obligability entailing the unacceptability of the OES supposition, in other words, an instance of the symmetry of the incompatibility relation. I suggest, however, that the paradoxical character of the denial of obligability is sufficient to tip the balance in favor of rejecting the OES supposition. Moreoever, while acknowledging the chicken-egg quality of the issue, we may recognize at least a *prima facie* case for the claim that a particular instance subsumed under a generalization is more strongly warranted than is the generalization itself (since the truth of the latter assures that of the former, but not vice versa). Thus, if we have a test of obligability which no action can satisfy, but have many actions which seem clearly obligable, it is not unreasonable to assume that this test simply fails to embody our standard of obligability. Still, it would seem helpful to say something about the basis of the initial plausibility of the OES supposition, and about our actual practice in distinguishing obligable from non-obligable actions.

Before turning to that task, it may be well to comment on a fact which may have struck the reader, namely, that mention of determinism/indeterminism appears to have dropped out of our discussion. The reason for this fact deserves mention. It is that reference in the Dilemma of Obligability to determinism or to indeterminism is basically vacuous. First, it should be obvious that it is not the truth of determinism alone which implies the non-obligability of actions − nor is it the truth of any form of indeterminism. Reaching the non-obligability conclusion requires the addition of a further premise. But since this added premise is the same whether we start from the assumption of determinism or from that of indeterminism − it is, of course, the OES supposition − it is this added premise which does all the real work. That is, since the conclusion that no action is or can be obligable follows from the OES supposition together with the assumption of the truth of determinism, and since it follows from the OES supposition together with the assumption of the falsity of determinism, i.e. the assumption of the truth of indeterminism, the non-obligability conclusion essentially follows from the OES supposition alone. But that supposition sets a standard of obligability which no action can satisfy, at least if the supposition is interpreted as requiring that an obligable action be one not having sufficient conditions traceable back to factors outside the agent's control.

Now we do, of course, attribute obligability and non-obligability; since such attribution involves moral judgment, we should not be surprised if we find no simple formula setting forth our criteria of obligability. But we can say generally, in terms of our ordinary criteria, that an agent is obligable for each of his actions unless there are circumstances attending the action which absolve him of obligability for it. Such conditions may be called *absolving conditions*. In the case of an action which is *prima facie* blameworthy, absolving conditions are naturally called *excusing conditions*. These are to be distinguished, incidentally, from *extenuating circumstances*, in that the latter merely serve to reduce the degree of blameworthiness for an action without eliminating the agent's obligability. Thus, there is a *presumption* of agent obligability with respect to any given action. (Consider: "I did it, *but* I don't deserve praise (blame) for my action.") But whether or not this presumption is outweighed in a given case is a matter of practical judgment, as is the determination of what qualifies as an absolving condition. Normally, of course, we count as absolving conditions only particular states of affairs, e.g., a person's coming down with a crippling disease, rather than some general characteristic of the universe, e.g., its being governed by causal laws. We may note, incidentally, that the presumption of obligability does the work which proponents of 'immanent causation' (discussed earlier) wish done by that notion, namely assigning obligability for actions to their agents — without the attendant difficulties or inadequacies of that notion. The tendency to take *persons* as the locus of responsibility is reflected, it would seem, in the primitive tendency to *personify* natural forces whose causal antecedents are unknown. Fortunately, the practice of scientific depersonalization, which involves, *inter alia*, seeing all entities equally as components in a chain of transeunt causation, need not be extended — for *all* purposes — to persons: there are, as we shall see, perfectly obvious reasons for attributing obligability to persons — in the absence, of course, of absolving conditions.

Absolving conditions are *obviously* certain matters of fact,

as, e.g., the fact that a person was unaware of the danger he
subjected himself to (and hence was not to be praised for his
courage) or the fact that a person was stricken with a disabling
disease (and hence was not to be blamed for failing to fulfill
an obligation). Now, if we do not wish to operate in an arbitrary
fashion in absolving persons of obligability (or, more generally,
in moral decision-making) it might appear that the remedy would
be in the determination of what various circumstances which
constitute absolving conditions have in common, taking the
common factor(s) as a criterion of excuse or absolution from
responsibility. We may seek, that is, to state in a general way
what makes a certain circumstance an absolving condition. It
would appear to be the attempt to satisfy this requirement which
has led to the generalization that 'ought' implies 'can'; i.e. to the
OES supposition: 'X couldn't have done otherwise' is taken as
a general formula to designate an absolving condition; hence to
say that someone couldn't have done otherwise is to say that
– since he is absolved of obligability – he is not obligable.

It is easy enough to see how one might be led to this generalization – many cases of non-obligability can be seen as cases
of non-substitutability – but it is equally easy to see that sub-
stititability is neither a necessary nor a sufficient condition of
obligability. I trust that the cases to which I apply the expression
'could (could not) have done otherwise' will be non-controversial
cases of substitutability (non-substitutability). Clearly, I will
not be using the (non-standard) standard of substitutability with
which we have hitherto been concerned, since, as we have seen,
it is a standard which no action could satisfy. Rather, insofar
as one attempted to give a (rough and ready) characterization
of the relevant test of the applicability of 'can' or 'could', it would
be one which (*pace* Austin?) is 'iffy': at least in many cases, the
test of whether or not an agent can, under given circumstances,
perform an action is provided by determining whether he does

perform it under those circumstances, if he is suitably motivated. We have seen above some of the difficulties of a hypothetical *analysis* of 'can' or 'could'; we shall see below the basis for the central importance of considerations of motivation for the attribution of obligability, considerations to which such an analysis, at least implicitly, points.

Let us assume that a person who fails to fulfill an obligation which he has voluntarily undertaken is *prima facie* — i.e., in the absence of an excusing condition — blameworthy. Suppose Jones borrows five dollars from Searle, promising to pay it back on the following Saturday. Suppose, further, that as Jones approaches Searle's house on Saturday, with the intention of repaying the debt, he is set upon by robbers who take all his money. Under those circumstances, not having five dollars, Jones would not, clearly, be able to pay Searle that sum of money, no matter how much he might wish to do so. And presumably in this case Jones' inability to fulfill the obligation would constitute an excusing condition. One can imagine all sorts of other cases in which one's inability to fulfill obligations, to hurt or help others (or oneself), and, in general, to do what one ought or ought not to do constitutes an absolving condition. Such inability may be due to any number of factors, including ignorance, disease, drugs, accident, and forcible confinement. But if these considerations tempt one to generalize about the nature of absolving conditions, then this is a temptation which is to be resisted, as consideration of two sorts of cases makes clear. One sort of case is that in which inability is not an absolving condition; the other is that in which one is to be absolved of obligability even though he could have done otherwise. Both sorts of cases are perfectly familiar.

The first sort can be illustrated by a slight variation on the story told above. It is perfectly obvious that in that story Jones would be unable to keep his promise to Searle if, on the Saturday in question, Jones did not have five dollars, regardless of the reason for this state of affairs. But although this reason does not affect the question of Jones' *ability* to fulfill his obligation, it assuredly does affect the question of his *obligability* (both with respect to its existence, and its degree). Thus, if we alter our original story so that the money is not forcibly taken from Jones, but rather, e.g., so that Jones spends the money to satisfy a silly whim, or Jones gambles the money away, or Jones carelessly loses the money, then Jones' inability to pay his debt would not constitute an excusing condition for his failure to do so. That is, in none of these cases would Jones be totally blameless. Thus, inability is not always an excusing condition. Presumably only an inability which itself is excusable excuses; but whether or not a particular instance of inability is to be excused is a matter for practical judgment and is not to be decided on the basis of a general formula.

Since this example is easily misunderstood, and, taken in isolation, readily countered, I should add a few comments on it. The example is forceful against the OES supposition inter- preted-naturally enough-so that obligability and substitutability are predicated of one and the same action (or omission). Suppose, for purposes of comparison, that one asserts the principle that performance implies ability: surely this should be taken as asserting that someone's *doing A* is a logically sufficient condition of that person's *being able* to do *A*. Similarly, that obligability implies substitutibility may be taken as meaning that *P*'s being able to do *A* or to refrain from doing *A* is a necessary condition of *P*'s being obligable for *A*, and the example is designed to counter that claim. Now the example may in turn be countered by the claim that Jones is not (really) obligable for failing to repay the loan but only for (the substitutable act of) bringing about his inability to do so. This sort of rejoinder is implausible on several counts. The most general response to it is that persons must surely be held obligable for readily foreseeable consequences of their actions, and Jones' inability (and subsequent) failure to repay the money is an obvious consequence of his squandering it. Moreover, in inexcusably losing the money, Jones becomes unable to do all sorts of things, e.g. to purchase innumerable different items costing five dollars. Yet, for these other inabilities he is clearly not obligable; it is only because he has an obligation to repay the loan that the question of his obligability for being able to do so even arises. Finally, if we consider the parallel case of a person who is unable to control the car he is driving because he is intoxicated and, as a result, kills a child, we surely hold the driver responsible not just for failing to control his car, but for killing the child as well.

A more common and more plausible counter to the example and to ones like it is this: Jones is indeed obligable for not repaying his debt even though he is unable to do so, but only because a necessary condition of his current inability is an earlier substitutable action of his. Thus, given the transitivity of the relation in question (*is a necessary condition of*), substitutability is, after all, a necessary condition of obligability. The principle appealed to is not that presupposed earlier, namely, that the obligability of action A requires the substitutability of A, but rather it is one which holds that obligability for A requires *either* the substitutability of A or the substitutability of some action (by the same agent) which is a necessary condition of the non-substitutability of A. Now, not only is this a plausible principle, but it is one which, I believe, holds in general. I shall postpone a discussion of why I believe that it fails to hold universally until Chapter IX, following a general discussion of practical principles in the next two chapters. Roughly, the idea is this: How strict a standard of obligability we are justified in upholding, i.e., the extent to which we are justified in disallowing excusing conditions, or absolving conditions in general, is a function of particular circumstances. In extreme circumstances we may be justified in disallowing as an excusing condition even non-substitutability of the sort indicated in the principle.

I should add, incidentally, that even if this argument is finally rejected, and it is maintained that substitutability (of some sort) is a presupposition of obligability, still this would not undermine the sort of compatibilist position supported by the example. In order to present a clear case of non-substitutability, I had to employ an instance in which an agent's action (omission) was not even hypothetically substitutable. (I.e., at the appointed time, Jones was unable to repay the debt even *if* he had wanted to.) At worst, then, hypothetical substitutability, despite its failure as the basis for an adequate analysis of '*P* could have done otherwise', may be the sort of substitutability required for obligability. Again, I want to deny even this weak claim, but even were it to be granted, it would provide no threat to compatibilism, since, as has frequently been noted, hypothetical substitutability appears to be quite consistent with determinism.

If inability (to do otherwise) is not a sufficient condition of non-obligability, neither is it a necessary condition. This can be readily seen if we consider a case of coercion in which the existence of a threat is agreed to constitute an absolving condition. The case may be, say, that of a bank official who hands over funds entrusted to him to individuals who have threatened bodily harm or death to his wife if he fails to do so. In an obvious sense, he could have done otherwise. Only he is excused, since it is thought unreasonable to have required, or even expected, the bank official to have risked harm to his wife under the circumstances in question. This case, incidentally illustrates a point which merits further comment.

The close association of ideas which has developed between the concepts of obligability and substitutability is shown by the fact that with respect to the imagined bank official – and in all sorts of other cases – we should be prepared to say that he was to be excused for what he did. Professor Richard Bronaugh, in a paper

which I much admire,[6] has claimed that the use of expressions
such as 'X could (not) have done otherwise' is (in practical contexts) the same as that of 'X did not (did) have an excuse'. Now
if we (thereby) identify substitutability with the absence of an
excuse and non-substitutability with the presence of one, and
take it as a 'tautology'[7] that one who has a proper excuse is not
obligable, it is easy to see how we preserve the OES supposition: if
non-substitutability *is* simply the presence of an excuse, and if the
latter entails non-obligability, then obviously non-obligability is a
logical consequence of non-substitutability. And, of course, taking
substitutability in this way, i.e., as involving moral evaluation of
the action in question, does not lead into the Dilemma of Obligability, as a more 'factual' interpretation of 'could have done
otherwise' appears to do. Thus, it appears that we can avoid this
Dilemma, *and* preserve the OES supposition if, and presumably
only if,[8] we tie substitutability to obligability in a manner such as
that which Bronaugh suggests. Now it seems to me that Bronaugh
is on firm ground in tying non-obligability to excuses, but on
much less firm ground in taking freedom (or substitutability) as
the absence of an excuse. 'Freedom (or substitutability) as the
absence of an excuse' has an odd ring about it which, to my ear,
at least, 'obligability (or responsibility) as the absence of an
excuse' does not. To be sure, as I have already indicated, we do
sometimes use 'couldn't do otherwise' to mark the existence of
excusing conditions, but the fact itself requires explanation. Part
of that explanation lies in the fact that not infrequently (factually
determinable) inability to perform or to refrain from performing
an action constitutes an excusing condition: (over-)generalization
of this sort of case leads to the OES supposition in a reading
relevant to the Dilemma of Obligability, and by a not unfamiliar
process of terminological change to the use of 'cannot' for all
sorts of excusing conditions which by no means literally involve
inabilities.[9]

It is worth noting, in attempting to see more clearly the relationship between 'oughts' and 'cans', that earlier it appeared to
be the close logical ties between obligability and substitutability
that led us into the Dilemma of Obligability; now it appears that
it is the closeness of these ties which enables us to bypass it.
The explanation of this apparent anomaly lies in the fact that
the two views involve a reversal in the roles of substitutability
and obligability as test conditions or independent variables. On
the earlier view, substitutability is taken as an independently
determinable fact about a given action, which is taken as a necessary condition of the action's obligability. On the sort of view
presently under consideration, 'X couldn't have done otherwise'
is, in effect a *façon de parler* indicative of, and dependent upon,
the presence of excusing conditions; in short, (non-)substitut-
ability. Now this view has the merit of accounting as we have
seen for our usage in one kind of case, but it fails to account
for those cases in which we excuse a person because he couldn't
do otherwise, or refuse to excuse him despite his inability to do
otherwise (since his inability is itself culpable). More importantly,
it has nothing to say with respect to that version of the OES
supposition which lies at the heart of the Dilemma of Obligability,
which takes it as obvious or as axiomatic that a person is not
obligable for an action for which there exist sufficient conditions
which can be traced back to factors outside the agent's control.

In any event, if, as I suggest, obligability for an action is constituted by absence of absolving conditions, then there is not
much point in trying to interpose substitutability as a mediating
condition. To be sure, *sometimes* inability to do otherwise *is*
an absolving condition, but if, out of deference to *one* sort of
colloquial usage, we *identify* substitutability with the absence
of such a condition, then not only do we fail to do justice to
other idiomatic uses, but we also, by preserving the OES supposition, maintain a principle with the demonstrated capability

of sowing confusion. At best reference to substitutability in connection with obligability is superfluous; at worst, it is highly misleading. Thus I deem it preferable to treat substitutability as a factually determinable condition — while noting, of course, that the colloquial use of expressions like 'he couldn't do otherwise' may involve no literal reference to non-substitutability (cf: 'God only knows', in ordinary speech, makes no theological reference) — and once and for all abandoning the OES supposition. Since the question of determinism has bearing on the free will problem only because of its relevance to (non-)substitutability, the resolution of that problem insofar as it is thought to involve a challenge to obligability involves the clear recognition of the conceptual independence of 'oughts' and 'cans'.

Let me add one last comment on the tendency to suppose that 'ought' implies 'can'. Often this tendency seems to depend on the apparent unreasonableness of holding a person responsible for failing to do that which he is unable to do. I have suggested that there are cases which show that this practice is not *always* unreasonable. It seems obvious that the correct principle is not that non-substitutability implies non-obligability, but only that *non-culpable* non-substitutability does, i.e., that if a person is not blameworthy or praiseworthy for his inability to perform or refrain from a given action, then he is not to be blamed or praised for (not) performing it. This weaker principle does not involve the apparent derivation of an 'ought' from an 'is', and, more importantly for present purposes, does not give rise to the dilemma of obligability, as does the stronger OES supposition.

In Chapter IX, I shall discuss the justification for what I take to be our practice in the ascription of obligability. Whether or not my account of our practice is correct, the justification of any practice, or indeed of any instance, of the ascription of obligability presupposes the existence of action, since the notion of obligability has application only to actions and their agents.

The claim that there are actions hardly requires proof: even to make (or to deny) the claim is to perform an action. And this last point seems to hold regardless of the truth or falsity of the deterministic thesis. I mention this issue only because it is sometimes suggested that the truth of determinism is incompatible with the occurrence of genuine actions. This suggestion seems sometimes based on an impoverished view of what is involved in the 'scientific world view' ('the molecules blindly run' etc.); the cure for this sort of misconception is the recognition of the richness of the natural world, and of the various sorts of causal explanation – social, psychological, biological, chemical, etc., etc. – which have been presented for different components or aspects of the world. That all these explanations – and the many which are constantly being developed – can be reduced to explanations in terms of physical principles – is hardly a proven thesis! But even if it is true, nothing is thereby destroyed: The 'higher level' concrete phenomena are surely not less *real* than the abstract theoretical entities of the physicist which, on this hypothesis, are supposed ultimately to explain them. Indeed, the reality of the phenomena to be explained is an obvious precondition of their being adequately explained.

Of primary importance for the question of attributing obligability to an agent is the possibility of higher level explanations of his actions in terms of his (motivating) reasons for acting, i.e., of his beliefs about and attitudes towards particular features (including, of course, consequences) of a contemplated action. On this point, I am in complete agreement with those who wish to draw a line between reasons and causes. We have seen above, however, that the arguments designed to show that reasons are not causes are unpersuasive, and, given the logical relations between bodily movements, which are admittedly subject to causal explanation, and actions, it would appear just as well that they are. As to why the presence of reasons for acting is of importance for the ascription of obligability, I shall have something to say in Chapter IX. Meanwhile, anyone who is worried that presenting causal explanations of actions will somehow destroy the actions can be reassured by the realization that such explanations presuppose not only the action to be explained, but also, in a somewhat different manner, the act of explaining. This last point is reminiscent of another worry of some who draw an overly sharp dichotomy between reasons for and causes of belief, a dichotomy based perhaps on a certain ambiguity in the notion of belief, the 'process-product' ambiguity. (On the one hand there are the propositional contents of belief, for which there are reasons — other propositions — but no causes; on the other, the acts or states of believing, or dispositions to believe, which may, of course, have non-rational causes, but which may be brought about — or caused — by consideration of reasons.) In any event, the worry is that what we take to be reasons for our beliefs will ultimately all be shown to be — in the light of advances in causal explanation — 'merely' causes. I need hardly point out the paradoxical quality of this sort of concern, the concern that scientific progress will give us adequate *reason* to believe that there are no reasons for our beliefs.

CHAPTER VII

UNPRINCIPLED MORALITY

We have seen that the OES supposition, on that reading in which it makes determinism/indeterminism relevant to the question of obligability, renders this last concept devoid of any possible application – as indeed C. D. Broad, for one, argued long ago.[1] This, it must be emphasized, is a purely conceptual point, and is independent of the extent to which events in our world are, or are found to be, subsumable under causal laws. Since we do in fact sometimes – indeed usually – consider persons' actions obligable, it is obvious that the OES supposition, however *prima facie* plausible it may be, fails to embody our actual test of obligability. This fact alone, of course, does not show that the practice of holding persons obligable is justified. A society may have quite definite rules determining which of its members are to be slaves and which slaveowners, and these rules may be generally accepted. A person's challenge of the institution of slavery is hardly shown to be unjustified by the fact that the challenger's moral standards differ from those commonly accepted. Obviously, we must distinguish the question of which institutions, practices, and actions are accepted, from that of which of these are justified, i.e., which ought to be accepted.

But the logical status of the practice of holding persons obligable is essentially different from that of holding persons enslaved with respect to the question of the justification of each. In the first place, to repeat a point suggested earlier, to justify a practice is to present sufficient reasons for the claim that it ought to be instituted or maintained: to justify the practice of holding persons obligable is to show that we ought to use 'ought' and 'ought not' with respect to some of their actions, and the denial of this claim appears incoherent. No such incoherence affects the justification of the abolition of slavery.

In the second place, it should be borne in mind that the suggestion under consideration, namely, that we abandon the practice of holding persons obligable, rests on the OES supposition, on a reading implying the impossibility of substitutability. This fact confronts us with a paradox: we engage in the practice of holding persons obligable; we should, it is suggested, abandon this practice, since obligability implies substitutability, and no actions are substitutable. But by the same token, the actions constitutive of the practice in question are non-substitutable; hence it is senseless to suggest that we ought to abandon them. These two claims of paradox are obviously related, although the second, by specifying the grounds (the OES supposition) which render the denial of obligability paradoxical will, I hope, dispel the air of merely verbal difficulty which may attend the first, and which might be thought capable of circumvention by such a device as that of saying that we ought now to bring it about that henceforth 'ought' and 'ought not' be not used, a suggestion which, however silly it may be, does not appear incoherent. But it does appear paradoxical to base such a recommendation on the OES supposition together with a non-referring notion of substitutability. Since on this account, no action could be obligable, it is senseless to use it to recommend that we *ought* to undertake a particular future course of action.

Perhaps, then, the practice of holding persons obligable needs no positive justification, since it has no coherent alternative. Still, there are familiar attempts at such justification based primarily on considerations connected with the social utility of the practice, and we shall look at them in Chapter IX, after some discussion of the nature of practical reasoning.

Meanwhile, it should be clear that what is of primary practical importance is not the abstract demonstration that some actions (or other) are obligable, but the determination of which actual actions are obligable and which are not. And, of course, if we succeed in the latter task, we *ipso facto* succeed in the former. But what can be said in a general way with respect to the obligability or non-obligability of particular actions seems very limited indeed. Failure adequately to recognize this limitation is an important source of the Dilemma of Obligability. We *can* say, it appears, that an action is obligable if − and, of course, only if − there is no absolving condition for the action. This formulation − while not *completely* unhelpful − takes us a very short way as far as the provision of a test for obligability goes. It merely converts *that* problem into one of determining what conditions are such as to absolve an agent of obligability, a problem which appears very resistant to solution on the basis of any general formula. We have seen how inadequate the claim that the agent couldn't do otherwise is as a general statement of absolving conditions. (The resolution of the free will puzzle consists largely in keeping this inadequacy clearly in mind.)

That the existence of absolving conditions for a given act rules out obligability for the act is a trivial truth. Since what constitutes an absolving condition is always some matter of fact, it may be tempting to suppose that by abstracting from the circumstances of non-obligable actions we can discover a general factual criterion of non-obligability. The one familiar attempt to find this criterion in the non-substitutability of actions has the anomolous consequence of denying obligability to every action. But it is to be doubted that any other factual consideration can provide an adequate test of non-obligability.

Perhaps one might hope for a test of obligability based on some common feature of actions which *are* obligable; i.e., without reference to the negative notions of absolving conditions or excuses. It is difficult to imagine what such a feature might be.

But more importantly, if there were such a feature it would be a general sufficient condition of the obligability of actions. It would thereby rule out the possibility of absolving conditions for the action in question — if it failed to do that it could not be an adequate criterion of obligability. Thus, it would seem that any discussion of the factual test-conditions or criteria of obligability might as well concern itself from the start with the notion of absolving conditions.

The concept of an absolving condition is extremely comprehensive — and admittedly vague — encompassing any feature which serves to render an agent non-obligable for an action he has performed (or omitted). To judge that there is something in a given situation which constitutes an absolving condition is to judge that a given agent ought not to be held accountable for a particular action, despite the general presumption of agents' obligability for their actions. Such a particular judgment is itself manifestly a practical judgment.

Now there seems widespread, though by no means universal, agreement on the view that one cannot formulate general principles on the basis of which deductively to justify particular practical judgments. Despite this apparent agreement, it will be useful, for purposes of understanding the nature of practical reasoning, to examine the considerations which lead to the expectation that there are, or must be such general principles, and then to note considerations which lead to the frustration of this expectation. Later, as I have suggested, I shall attempt to apply some of these general considerations to the question of the justification of the practice of holding persons obligable.

Although the moral skeptic obviously shares my doubts about the existence of general principles, my doubts are not based on moral skepticism. This is a view, incidentally, which seems no more to be maintained in practice than is, e.g., skepticism about the existence of the external world, and one which, like the latter, depends on an appeal to excessively high — indeed logically unmeetable — standards of what, for the area in question, constitutes justified belief. Nor are my doubts based on moral relativism, a view which — either in spite of, or because of a fair amount of consideration — I am by no means certain that I understand, in this regard (*inter alia*) being the inferior of practically every college sophomore, including myself when young. The view appears to have two components, and there are difficulties with both. The first is the factual claim that different individuals or groups have different fundamental standards of value. Now this may well be true, but it is by no means so obvious as it may appear to individuals when they first recognize that different individuals, or groups, make different evaluations of the same things (or states of affairs, or actions). Demonstrating that these differing evaluations are based on different standards of value requires showing that the objects of the evaluations are perceived in the same way; otherwise their being differently evaluated may result from different factual beliefs about them, rather than from different standards of value applied to them.[2] But even if this difficulty is overcome, a more paradoxical one remains. The second component of moral relativism, as I (mis)understand the doctrine, is an evaluative claim based on the factual one. What this claim apparently *intends* is the denial of moral superiority to either, or to any, of competing moral standards. Unfortunately, the making of such an evaluative claim itself presupposes a non-relative moral standard. Since I am not primarily concerned with moral relativism, I shall not pursue this (apparent) paradox. My concern about moral principles is based more on the possibility of conflict between *them*, than it is on the possibility of conflict between persons or groups who hold them.

Although the impossibility of formulating general principles adequate for the justification of particular practical judgments is, as I have suggested, a point which is widely accepted, the reason for this impossibility is by no means as widely agreed upon. Sometimes the claim of impossibility seems to be based on the belief which underlies much moral skepticism, that a practical 'judgment' represents nothing more than a feeling or an attitude towards a given action, and that the whole notion of practical *reasoning* is misguided, expect insofar as this notion applies to the determination of what one ought to do *if* he wishes to attain a given end. On this view, reason has a role in the appraisal of actions only insofar as they are considered as means to a given end (actual or imagined); for the rest, evaluation − including that of the ends − is a matter of feeling or attitude. Now any adequate account of practical reasoning must, it seems to me, take into account the importance of attitudinal factors in the making of practical judgments (over and above the importance they have in the making of *any* judgments).

But while a satisfactory account of practical reasoning must be alive to the role of attitudinal and other non-cognitive factors, it must also obviously be aware of the role of evaluative *reasons*. Consideration of this last point leads naturally to an explanation of the temptation to suppose that practical reasoning must be dependent on universal principles, and also to an account of why this temptation is to be resisted. At the heart of this account lies the familiar consideration that value concepts and value claims are supervenient or consequential, i.e., that these concepts or claims depend for their applicability or validity on straight-forwardly factual factors on which they 'supervene'. Value terms apply or fail to apply in virtue of facts; if relevant facts were different then a different value judgment would − or at any rate might − be warranted. This point is obvious: whether an action is right or wrong is dependent on the nature of the action; whether a state of affairs is good or bad is a function of its factual char-acteristics. Similarly for any value concept: just, courageous, rude, unpleasant, etc. So close, indeed, is this dependence, that in many cases there is no sharp distinction to be drawn between fact and value notions, since the presence of certain factual characteristics may be logically decisive for the applicability of terms we employ to express valuations. Thus, given a certain description of an action, it may no longer be an open question whether the action is an instance of lying, or courage, of adultery, of rudeness (Foot), and so on, and these are all value notions. It would not be fruitful, I think, to claim that these notions are really 'mixed' (part factual and part valuational), and that we can distinguish two different aspects in their employment, only one of which (the factual) follows logically from the factual description. To an ethical 'naturalist', one who supposes that value terms can be defined on the basis of descriptive terms, or, at least, that value judgments follow logically from factual ones, this cannot but appear a completely *ad hoc* distinction.[3]

Allowing then, at least for the sake of argument, that factual considerations may be quite decisive for many assertions which would normally be called value judgments, it still does not follow that such considerations are decisive with respect to those which I have called categorical practical judgments, i.e., judgments about what ought to be done, all things considered. Thus, suppose that a description of a certain action is granted to be sufficient for the determination that the action was rude. It hardly follows from this fact that the action ought not to have been performed. This negative verdict can be defeated in two ways: one can show that 'ought not' fails to apply either because the action was not obligable — i.e., that neither 'ought' nor 'ought not' applies to it, or because — despite its rudeness, the actions ought nonetheless to have been performed (or even that a little rudeness was just what was called for: perhaps, e.g., in the circumstances politeness to an evil and powerful individual would have constituted groveling). In the first sort of case, the action is not one which *ought not* to have been performed by the agent, since though it is perhaps untoward, it has an excusing condition, say, non-culpable ignorance of a peculiar local custom.[4] In the second, the *prima facie* wrongness which the action has in virtue of one characteristic is overridden by other features of the action. These cases exemplify the familiar distinction between excuse and justification. Less familiar – as shown by the absence of suitable terminology for it – is the analogous distinction which is applicable to actions denominated by expressions used to make favorable evaluations, such as 'polite', 'courageous', etc. We don't *excuse* someone for performing a polite action, even when he is not obligable with respect to it (I have, of course, been using 'absolving condition' to cover both 'excuse' and its analogue). And there is obviously wanting an analogue of 'justify' for cases such as those in which, e.g., other considerations override the courageous character of an action so that overall the action – despite this feature – ought not to have been performed. It is worth noting that the kinds (if any) of defenses (excuses and justifications) and their analogues available for given actions are in part dependent on the description or classification of the actions. As one result, it is not possible to draw a sharp line between excuses and justifications. Thus, suppose that an employee hands over funds entrusted to his care on threat of death to his wife. If we see the action as simply handing over the funds, we may find the action untoward, but with an external consideration which *excuses* its agent. If on the other hand, we see it as a case of saving a life by surrendering the funds we may see it as an action which is overall *justified* in that an aspect having disvalue is outweighed by others having positive value.

The possibility of overriding evaluations, either on the basis of absolving conditions or on the basis of factors justifying reevaluation, is central to practical reasoning. But, it may be urged, if practical *reasoning* is to have any claim to being so-called, there must be criteria in terms of which to weigh the claim that one consideration overrides another. That is, even if it is granted that particular kinds of evaluations, e.g., that actions are rude or courageous, may be insufficient to determine generally that they ought (not) to be done, there must be general criteria for deciding when these considerations are insufficient, on pain of making such decisions arbitrary. The criteria for ranking evaluations of actions may involve the lexical ordering[5] of classes of actions, such that any member of a given class is to be ranked above every member of a succeeding class. As Rawls admits,[6] and as I shall argue further below, the plausibility of such an ordering is not great. Moreover, to one seeking principles of ordering, any ordering of classes of actions which is itself not based on a single principle, must appear capricious. Thus, anyone who requires that for counting practical judgments as *rational*, they must be based on general principles, must require a general criterion for the valuational ordering either of *kinds* of actions or, directly, of particular actions. Such a requirement seems a prescription for moral skepticism: by setting too high a standard for rationality it assures that every moral judgment will count as irrational. (But as usual, when skepticism has done its work, there are still practically important distinctions to be drawn: if no practical judgment is *rational*, still some are more reasonable, or less unreasonable, than others.) To see something of the role of criteria in practical reasoning, and of how this role tends to become exaggerated, let us pick up the thread of our account at the point where we were remarking on the supervenient character of value notions (and of value assertions). This supervenience characterizes not just the more specific value characteristics, which we discussed above, but the most general, such as being just, good, bad, right, wrong, etc. Thus, an action is, say, right, in virtue of certain of its characteristics, its so-called right-making characteristics. Now since its rightness depends just on its right-making characteristics, any other action which had precisely those

characteristics and no other morally relevant features would also
— *ipso facto* — be right. This trivial truth, that the justified attribution of particular value properties to something is dependent
on that thing's possession of certain factual attributes is, it seems
to me, the basis of what is clearly *rational* in evaluative judgments
in general and in practical judgments in particular. It is what
establishes a requirement of a kind of consistency in such judgments, so that one is not free rationally to make moral judgments
ad libitum: such judgments are subject to the constraint of rational
criticism. Again, on pain of a tendency to skepticism, one must
not make too much of the claims of reason: reason, alone, e.g.
cannot tell us even that a certain factual consideration counts
in favor of a certain practical claim. Thus, consider the claim that
doing *A* will make certain persons happy constitutes a reason for
doing *A*: this claim itself involves a practical assessment. If, e.g.,
someone thinks that only the claims of a particular class of people
— say, members of a certain national, racial, or religious group,
or even that class of which the person in question is the sole
member — are of practical relevance, then that person's error
is moral, rather than logical, in character. Reason demands that
cases which are alike in relevant respects be judged alike — it does
not of itself tell us which respects are relevant. It is conceivable
that different individuals might hold internally consistent but
mutually incompatible sets of practical judgments, although one
suspects that the extent to which this theoretical possibility is
actually realized has been greatly exaggerated by ethical relativists,
given especially that actual practical judgments are developed
within the set of constraints necessitated by living in a civil society,
and in individuals who presumably start life with fundamental
similarities of genetic structure. To the extent that this possibility
is realized, however, to that extent *rational* persuasion of one
individual by another with regard to moral judgments is ruled out,
and this state of affairs may be thought to constitute one of moral

relativism. Three points should be noted. First, it has not been shown to what extent, if any, the possibility in question *is* realized. Second, if *relativism* is a doctrine about the *truth* of conflicting claims, then the impossibility of persuasion — rational or other — is hardly a sufficient condition for its justification. Finally, if the impossibility of the rational resolution of conflicting claims is the ground for relativism, the moral relativist owes us a demonstration that such impossibility peculiarly affects *moral* claims.

I have spoken rather freely of moral or practical *principles*, and this manner of speaking may well lead to a misleading view of the nature of practical reasoning. Not to be misled, one must recognize — and, of course, keep in mind — the limitations, as well as the scope of moral generalizations. It is, as we have seen, trivially true, that if a given action is right, then any other action just like it in all relevant respects is *ipso facto* right. The reference to 'relevant respects' is apposite for two reasons, (a) without some restriction of characteristics in which morally like actions must be similar, the generalization arising from our 'trivial truth' would be empty, since no two actions are alike in all respects, and (b) most features which could be used to characterize the action — e.g. the day of the week on which it was performed, the eye color of its agent, etc. — are normally not relevant to its moral character. Now consider any action correctly adjudged to be right — it has some set of relevant characteristics C which make it right, and so we may take it as an abstract principle that whatever is C is right. This is not, I think, incorrect. But if it suggests that there are practical principles adoption of which can eliminate the necessity of making particular moral *judgments*, then it is quite misleading. Suppose that a particular action is right simply because it is a case of promise-keeping, i.e., since the only (positive) feature which is relevant for its practical evaluation is that performing the action would involve keeping a promise. From this, it seems to follow that all acts of promise-keeping are right. But obviously this won't do. For suppose that for some other action, the correct judgment is that it is wrong, and the basis for this judgment — and the only morally relevant fact about it — is that its performance will cause pain to someone. This yields the principle that all actions which cause pain are wrong. But there are familiar cases in which my keeping a promise will cause pain. (I may have promised *A* to tell him a painful truth, or to harm *B*, or whatever); our talk of *principles* in these cases appears to lead to the conclusion that such actions are both right and wrong.

We can seek to avoid this conclusion in a number of ways, without abandoning appeal to principles in justifying particular moral judgments. We can claim that in one or both such cases the principle appealed to has been incompletely specified; we can claim that the principles themselves can be ordered in terms, perhaps, of a higher-order principle: or we can claim that there is a principle underlying the particular practical judgments we make, but that our description of this generalization is (not so much incomplete as) insufficiently general. None of these approaches is particularly promising. By the first claim, I mean the view that promise-keeping is a relevant feature in determining that an action is right, but that any principle embodying that feature must incorporate, as exceptions, whatever features may override the claim of rightness. Thus, if the principle of promise-keeping is thought to have exceptions built into it so that it becomes "an act of promise-keeping is right unless its performance causes too much pain or ... ", we may avoid the conclusion that a given action is both right and wrong. But we hardly have anything recognizable as a *principle*. In the first place, it is by no means clear that the kinds of exceptions lend themselves to specification, i.e., that there won't be further sorts of cases to be added to any list we may make. But more importantly, what this sort of procedure does is to shift the burden of assessing the weight of various considerations so that one must make such an assessment in order to determine that the 'principle' applies to a given case. That is, a principle, so formulated, does not obviate the need for particular moral judgments, since such judgments are required for determining the very applicability of the principle in a particular instance.

The second alternative, that a conflict of reasons or considerations applicable to a given case is to be resolved by an ordering ('lexical') of the principles in question. This view is suggested by such claims as these: the principle of preventing harm takes precedence over that of doing good, preventing injustice has an absolute priority over concern for consequences, moral considerations take absolute precedence over non-moral considerations. That there can be a reasonable lexical ordering of all (kinds of) practical principles, or even that we can talk intelligibly of *all* such principles is vastly improbable. But even that it is reasonable to expect a lexical ordering with respect to *any* two principles is doubtful. We may waive the point that if principles can be evaluated apart from a (higher-order) principle, then the question of why particular actions cannot *also* be evaluated directly, i.e. without appeal to general principles, will surely suggest itself. The basis of our present concern is that particular reasons of a given kind, subsumable under a single principle, obviously differ in strength. Thus, some obligations – or some obligations of a particular sort, e.g., to keep a promise – may be more 'stringent' than others, i.e., they may be less easily overridden by opposing considerations. Similarly for different cases of considerations in favor of the claim that an action ought to be performed, when these cases fall under a single principle: some will support the practical judgment more strongly than others. But this fact renders the possibility of 'prioritizing' principles dubious indeed. For this possibility implicitly assumes that a reason of a certain kind – no matter how vanishingly small its weight – must somehow take precedence over considerations of another sort, no matter how weighty: it tells us, e.g., not only to let justice be done though the heavens fall, but to accept this consequence no matter how minor the injustice thereby averted.

Again, if reasons of a single kind are in conflict (as, e.g., considerations of justice may conflict in the proposed hiring of one individual as opposed to another, and, more generally, *moral* considerations may obviously be in opposition in this and in many other kinds of cases), then the acceptance of lexical ordering will prohibit consideration of reasons of a less favored kind (e.g. ones involving considerations of consequences, or of prudential factors) no matter how weighty, and will do so no matter how closely balanced the considerations of the favored kind may be. This is clearly absurd.

Nor will appeal to higher-order principles which justify our moral principles remedy the situation. Normally such principles are not thought of as providing a rule for ordering the lower-order principles or maxims. Thus, under 'rule utilitarianism' the maxims of promise-keeping, truth-telling, prohibition of murder, etc. are *each* thought of as justified by considerations of utility, but so construed this doctrine is not helpful in evaluating an action which involves a conflict of maxims, just the sort of case where help may be wanted. Traditionally, when confronted with this difficulty, utilitarians such as Mill have 'reverted' to act utilitarianism, i.e., to the evaluation of a particular act on the basis of *its* utility, rather than on the basis of the utility of general adherence to some maxim which the act instantiates.[7] We may note in passing that one of the obvious difficulties with rule utilitarianism, as with other doctrines which depend on the identification of *the* maxim or principle of a given action, is that any action can be described in many ways, and, hence, can be brought under many different principles, not all of which need be evaluated alike in terms of the higher-order principle (utility, universalizability) being employed. If we assume — not too plausibly, perhaps — that we can in some non-arbitrary manner decide which features of actions are constitutive of maximhood, we confront the difficulty of conflict of principles just noted. And if, to avoid this conflict, we think of the higher-order principle as ordering maxims, then we have in exacerbated form the implausibility of lexical priority of maxims. This implausibility is exacerbated simply because not only, as we have seen, in evaluating an action the smallest weight of a consideration of one sort takes absolute precedence over the greatest weight of a consideration of a sort with lower priority, but also because in our evaluation of the action, consideration of the sort of concern on which the lexical ordering is itself based is ruled out. Thus, for example, if maxims are lexically ordered on the basis of the estimated utility resulting from their general adoption, then if applying this ordering yields an intuitively implausible or doubtful result in a particular case, we are precluded from considering the probable utility of the individual action, on pain of sullying the purity of our principles. It is difficult to conceive of a credible principle of evaluation for either particular actions or for the ordering of maxims which totally ignored consideration of consequences. Indeed, not many general higher-order principles for the evaluation of maxims come to mind: apart from rule utilitarianism, there are (Kantian) universalizability, and, of course, divine command. Since a given maxim is either universalizable or not, universalizability is not a device for the evaluative *ordering* of maxims. And even if divine command were to provide a lexical ordering of moral maxims, it is obviously an ordering that could be superseded (by divine command) in a particular case. (In a later chapter I shall discuss the possibility of divine command as the basis for practical evaluation.) It appears then that lexical ordering of evaluative principles or maxims is a very dubious undertaking, and that its plausibility is, if anything, diminished if thought of as accomplished on the basis of higher-order principles.

Now seeing the implausibility of lexical ordering of evaluative principles is not of great importance in itself, since no one is much concerned with such a project. But this implausibility appears of greater significance when it is realized that the rejection of lexical ordering of principles or maxims is, in effect, the rejection of the possibility of basing practical evaluations on the appeal to general principles, and this rejection, as we have seen, may be taken as the essential claim of ethical intuitionism.

If a particular evaluation is to be based on appeal to a principle, then that principle must not be subject to defeat by appeal to some other principle which may be overriding in a particular case. This outcome can be attained by attempting a principled ordering of maxims, a procedure of dubious feasibility, or by attempting to find a single principle which is decisive in the evaluation of any given action. If there is such a principle, it clearly must be one involving some feature that characterizes every human action, or at least every action subject to potential evaluation. This fact obviously rules out all sorts of maxims from consideration as this fundamental principle; e.g. that one ought to tell the truth is a maxim applicable only to actions involving speech, or speech-like behavior. Now whether or not there are other practically relevant features characterizing all actions, at least one such feature of all actions is that they have *consequences*, i.e., like all other events, they have some effect, however slight, on the world. It is therefore tempting to suppose that a single-valued principle of evaluation should be a form of *consequentialism*, the view that consideration of consequences is alone decisive in the evaluation of an action. This view yields a single principle only when a single sort of consequence is singled out, where a *single sort* of consequence is one such that the determination that an action has such a consequence does not require an independent evaluative judgment. The point of this last proviso is to rule out speaking of a single kind of consequence, e.g. human happiness, when the 'single kind' involves components with themselves may involve evaluative conflict. Thus, e.g. Mill, having, with Bentham, equated happiness with pleasure, and having told us that happiness is the sole end of actions and therefore (!) the sole criterion of their rightness, when confronted with the question of whether other things, e.g. virtue or money, may not be intrinsically good had in all candor to admit that they are. But he tried to avoid inconsistency by saying that these goods, which start by being sought as a means to happiness or pleasure, end up as being 'parts of' happiness. (Indeed it is not clear that Mill genuinely distinguishes between being sought for its own sake and being part of happiness.) Such verbal legerdemain serves unfortunately to destroy one of the obvious potential advantages of utilitarianism, namely that it provides a factual criterion, however difficult in practice to apply, for moral judgments. Thus if an action satisfies conflicting moral rules of thumb, then we resolve the conflict by testing the action in terms of the maximum happiness criterion. But if the considerations embodied in the rules of thumb are themselves built into the notion of happiness, then such a resolution is ruled out. Thus, suppose one course of action will effect a maximization of political liberty; a second, a maximization of knowledge; and a third, a maximization of wealth. How are we to choose among them? Well, on one familiar version of classical utilitarianism we adopt that course of action which will maximize the balance of happiness (= pleasure) over unhappiness (= pain) or minimize the balance of unhappiness over happiness. And, waiving, for the sake of argument, all the (unsurmountable) difficulties with respect to ambiguities in 'pleasure' and 'pain', and with respect to placing all pleasures and all pains on a single scale among themselves and with each other, this would yield a single moral criterion. But this advantage of utilitarianism is lost when considerations of other sorts — which may, and do, themselves conflict — are built into our definition of 'happiness', or of whatever else we may take as embodying our 'single' criterion of practical evaluation.

It seems otiose to *argue* that there can be no adequate single principle of practical judgments, i.e., one that obviates the need for *judgment* (or moral 'intuition'). That there *must* be such a single principle is a belief arising from the correct observation that moral considerations are implicitly general, which, indeed, is what makes them significantly describable as *reasons* (these reasons being, of course, evaluative, not necessarily motivational). But, that a certain action ought to be performed shows only that reasons for its performance exist, and that none of sufficient weight to override these exist; not that none would – under different circumstances – exist. A general *principle* could capture the implicit universality of the moral judgment only by specifying all *possible* considerations which would defeat that judgment, were they to obtain.

Hedonistic utilitarianism – taking seriously something like Bentham's hedonistic calculus as its basis – is perhaps the principal historical theory to provide such a principle. Bentham may well be right in claiming that the sole alternative to his principle of utility – apart from that of 'asceticism' – is the principle of 'sympathy and antipathy', i.e., no principle at all.[8] We can bypass the familiar difficulties with pleasure and pain, some of which have been suggested above, by imagining a world arising from our own, and one which appears to embody the hedonistic ideal. Concerning it we may wonder whether it represents a worthy goal for the long historical period of human toil, frustration, aspiration, and suffering. This world, little different in essentials from numerous other imaginary ones which have been conjured up since the time of Homer, is one in which brains are developed which are capable of surviving outside bodies ('disembodied brains') with the ability to reproduce themselve rapidly and to survive by metabolizing whatever free (i.e., not attached to another

brain) chemical elements are in the vicinity. This ongoing meta-
bolic process serves to stimulate a pleasure center in the brain.
These brains expand throughout the universe, destroying all
other sentient life — we may suppose that being consumed by
brain(s) is also an experience of ecstatic pleasure. Here, with
perhaps a few embellishments, is a hedonistic utopia, but I suspect
no one would think of it as desirable, even if the original brains
from which the others derived were human — so that it could
be said that human pleasure was being maximized, although it
is not clear why the distinction between human and other pleasure
should matter to a hedonist.

   This mad story not only provides an allegory about utopias
which involve remaking humankind — and which do not? — but
more mundanely, it is instructive with respect to the concept
of intrinsic goods. Such goods, at least since Plato, have been
contrasted with instrumental goods, the latter being 'good' only
as a means to something else, which is thought of as desirable
for its own sake. Indeed, it was thought that the existence of the
distinction showed that there *must* be things which are desirable
for their own sakes; an intrinsic good came to be construed as
something ·which would be desirable if it existed all alone, i.e.,
if nothing else existed other than the intrinsically valuable thing.[9]
But, as our story should make clear, the distinction of instrumental and non-instrumental value supports no such claim. For
though pleasurable sensations are not sought (merely) as a means
to anything else, it does not follow that they would be desirable
if they existed by themselves. The dichotomy of being desired as a
means, or being desired for its own sake, is clearly not exhaustive:
we can, e.g., desire something as a *component* of something else.
And, of course, this is just how we do normally desire things:
we tacitly assume an entire context of human life in which the
objects we pursue are worth pursuing; it is only in such a context
that anything has value. This is at least part of the reason for

the failure to find a kind of goal to provide a single criterion of moral evaluation.

Clearly we need not rely on a wild science-fiction story to show the inadequacy of taking the maximization of pleasure as the sole criterion for practical evaluation. Indeed it is conceivable that someone might think the world described in the story is a very good one, and one in which he would like to have himself — i.e., his brain — participate! Some of the more mundane — and familiar — objections to supposing that there could be a single criterion for evaluating actions based on their consequences — and it is clear that there cannot be such a principle which totally ignores these consequences — are of two sorts. First there are the objections resting on the obvious fact that there is no single kind of instrinsic good, except, again, a 'single' kind which has (potentially) conflicting components. But beyond these are objections based on the fact that even if there were just one kind of intrinsic good, this would still not be sufficient for a single moral principle. For there would still be conflicting *prima facie* principles involving the intrinsic good in question. One such principle is that usually identified with *utilitarianism*, namely, that we ought to act so as to *maximize* the good. But this principle may conflict with other principles bearing on the *distribution* of the good. Thus, since we are dealing, *ex hypothesi* with the *sole* intrinsic good, there is presumably some *minimum* amount of the good to which everyone is entitled. Distinct from the question of a minimum for each, there are other questions of desert of or justice in distribution. Since an overwhelming proportion of the determinants of this distribution as it now occurs — both within and between different societies — appears to be a matter of chance, many see distributive justice as involving a tendency toward equality in the distribution of goods, even though such a tendency may run counter to maximization of the goods. Others may see the notion of desert or justice as having application only within a system of societal rules of a contractual sort, although, of course, there may be constraints, utilitarian or other[10] on what rules are acceptable. In Chapter Five of *Utilitarianism*, Mill points out a number of conflicting notions of distributive justice, all of which are, to some degree, intuitively appealing. He sees utilitarianism as being required to mediate among them. Unfortunately it is by no means clear how this mediation is supposed to be accomplished; indeed if utilitarianism is taken as a principle involving the *maximization* of whatever is intrinsically good, it is a position standing in direct opposition to our central notions of distributive justice.[11]

Another sort of difficulty with any form of consequentialist view, and, indeed, with consequentialism in general, is one which may be related to the difficulties of the lexical ordering of practical reasons. Let us make the implausible − not to say impossible − assumption that we have formulated a single criterion of intrinsic good involving a notion of satisfaction, or pleasure, or whatever, and which somehow takes into account the various considerations involved in the distribution of that good. On this criterion, if one course of action yields a greater balance of this good than does another, then the former ought to be − indeed is required to be − undertaken, regardless of the amount of the difference of good to be realized, and regardless of any other possible considerations. Thus, in effect, if there are other factors to be considered, they are lexically posterior to those of satisfaction/pleasure. Perhaps they will enter in, e.g., when considerations of the latter sort resulting from two proposed courses of action balance out. Thus, if two courses of action will yield an equal amount of pleasure/ satisfaction suitably distributed throughout the affected population, then (and only then) we may choose one of the courses of action on the ground, say, that it will yield a greater degree of political freedom. One who was blindly in love with a utilitarian theory could deny that freedom was even a *prima facie* intrinsic good, claiming that the value of freedom, as of everything else other than satisfaction, is purely instrumental. But if freedom is a consideration which comes into play when the lexically prior consideration of satisfaction does not apply, then we face another instance of the peculiar difficulty of the notion of lexical priority. It is simply not credible that if freedom is a *prima facie* good, that then a large balance of freedom should not outweigh even the smallest balance of unhappiness or discontent. As a matter of fact, of course, we claim that we are willing to accept a great deal of unpleasantness for the sake of political freedom.

Quite similar comments apply to consequentialism in general. If one supposes that consideration of consequences must always be decisive in rational practical evaluation, then he must recognize that there may be cases in which there is little or nothing to choose between the value of the consequences of two alternative courses of action. May we not in such cases take into account non-consequential (deontological) considerations? Surely the fact that one course of action involves telling a lie counts against its performance, while the fact that another would be a case of keeping a promise counts in its favor. But if these are evaluative reasons — and, of course, they are — then they have *some* weight in cases where the balance of consequential considerations opposes them, and they may often be reasonably adjudged to outweigh such considerations. As a matter of fact, we normally judge that it takes rather extreme consequential considerations to justify breaking a promise or telling a lie. Mark Twain was *joking* when he told the politician, "When in doubt, tell the truth".

It is a familiar fact that excessive concern for consequential at the expense of deontological considerations presents an ever-present temptation — and not just to persons holding positions of power. Such excessive concern is dangerous, i.e., it has undesirable *consequences*. But it is not to be remedied by ruling out consideration of consequences altogether when deontological considerations, or even certain kinds of deontological considerations, apply. No one would now say, I imagine, that one ought never to lie, regardless of consequences. There is no need at this point to go through the arguments against this extreme anti-consequentialism,[12] since they are parallel to those against consequentialism. Suppose that we claim that a certain class of actions ought (not) to be performed just in virtue of their possessing some non-consequential feature. We may note against this claim, that non-consequential features may be of relatively little weight, as involving a 'white lie', or a minor injustice; they may be outweighed, or at least counterbalanced, by other non-consequential considerations, as when keeping a promise involves telling a lie, or when being compassionate involves acting unjustly; and, of course, since consequences are not inconsequential, the deontological or non-consequential features may be simply outweighed by consideration of consequences.

Pace Miss Anscombe, this last point is not a reversion to consequentialism, since the non-consequential features may well outweigh the consequential ones, and indeed certain kinds, e.g., avoiding the judicial punishment of the innocent, almost invariably do. An ambiguity in the use of 'consequentialism' may tend to support the supposition that if consideration of consequences is always relevant in assessing an action, then this consideration must always be decisive. After all, the consequences of an action presumably extend indefinitely into the future and affect to some degree an indefinitely large number of sentient beings. If each of these effects carries some evaluative weight, then cumulatively consideration of consequences is bound to outweigh other sorts of considerations. This argument is not conclusive, since it does not show that there is a cumulative tendency of these effects of an action towards a favorable or towards an unfavorable evaluation. But more important from a practical standpoint are the obvious facts that a reasonable judgment can be based only on available information and that the overwhelming balance of information concerning the effects of our potential actions is not available to us at the time we decide to perform them. If we limit the notion of consequentialism by restricting the consequences relevant for the evaluation of a given action either to those intended by the agent, those expected by the agent, those that should reasonably have been expected by the agent, or whatever, then the fear that considerations of consequences will always be decisive in our practical evaluations should dissolve.[13]

If the central tenet of Ethical Intuitionism is that particular moral judgments cannot be justified by appeal to universal principles, but must be made and validated at least in part on the basis of the practical insight, judgment, or 'intuition' of the judger, then the point of view suggested by the foregoing arguments against the appeal to moral principles may be characterized as a form of intuitionism.[14] Since these arguments have been presented in a disjointed manner it is perhaps well to summarize them before attempting to indicate the role of reason in moral evaluation, which role the characterization of 'intuitionism' may seem to eliminate, or at least to downgrade excessively.

Fundamental to the possibility of the rationality of practical judgments, as for value judgments in general, is the supervenient character of value concepts and value judgments. This implies that a value characteristic holds or fails to hold in a given case in virtue of certain non-value or factual characteristics. But if value characteristics hold in virtue of factual characteristics, then not only is there a conceptual connection between instances of the two kinds of characteristics, but there is also a kind of irrationality or inconsistency involved in evaluating differently cases which are not — in relevant ways — factually different. These considerations may suggest the notion of valuational *principles*, general statements of the relevant factual considerations in virtue of which a given value characteristic holds. Now, depending on how broadly we interpret the notion of *value*, there may well be

such principles. Indeed there may be some which are analytic:
assuming that to call a given speech-act a *lie* is to *evaluate* it
(negatively), we may call it a valuational principle that if anyone
deliberately utters a statement which he knows to be false with
the intent of deceiving another, then he is lying. Perhaps there are
other exceptionless value generalizations which are not analytic,
e.g., that actions describable in a certain way (as, say, the judicial
punishment of one known to be innocent) are *ipso facto unjust*.
But since our concern is with practical judgments, i.e., with
judgments that some course of action ought or ought not (categorically) to be followed, we are concerned with the possibility
of *practical* principles. The application of other value principles
which enable us to evaluate certain factual elements of a situation
as being, say, courageous, unjust, or a lie, may provide a useful
auxiliary service in the making of a practical judgment. But
however it may be with other value judgments, it seems clear
that categorical practical judgments involve *judgment*, i.e., are
not to be decided by appeal to general practical principles, since
there can be no such principles. At best, a practical 'principle'
will embody an evaluative reason, a general consideration *pro*
or *contra* the performance of a given action. This reason may
involve a brute fact, as, e.g., that the action will cause pain or
healing or an institutional fact, as, e.g., that the action will involve
breaking a promise[15] or an (intermediate) evaluation, as, e.g.,
that the action will be courteous or unjust. But in a particular
situation, a given reason may have to be weighed against other,
competing, reasons. For this and other reasons, we cannot hope to
be able to base practical judgments on universally valid principles.
The generally useful metaphor of *weighing* considerations (on
which I shall say more in the next chapter) involves, incidentally,
a *suggestio falsi*, that of the commensurability of evaluative
reasons. Recognition of their incommensurability should rule out
the hope of generally grading reasons on the basis of a higher-order
principle embodying a single standard. Moreover, since it is obvious

that different considerations of the same kind, e.g., different consequential considerations, or different consequential considerations of a certain kind, say, those involving the maximization of pleasure, or different deontological considerations, or different deontological considerations of a certain kind, say, those involving promise-keeping, do have different evaluative weight, there is no point in attempting to formulate a general lexical ordering of kinds of reasons. Overlap seems inevitable, no matter how 'kind of evaluative reason' is defined.

The upshot of this undoubtedly overlong discussion — overlong, in that its conclusion might well have been granted by most readers without lengthy argument — is that what normally are counted as evaluative reasons are at best *prima facie* reasons, i.e., reasons for or against particular practical judgments which are capable of being overridden by opposed considerations. Hence, we see the important role of judgment ('intuition') in the evaluation of practical judgments: if we rule out appeal to universally valid moral principles, then we must rely on individual judgment in weighing conflicting reasons. Even, moreover, if there were no seriously conflicting reasons with respect to a given action, we might have to weight the relative merits and emerits of *alternative* courses of action. ('Might', of course, since we do not live our lives in a state of constant moral doubt or conflict.) In addition, it is worth remembering that the determination that some consideration *is* an evaluative reason is itself not a matter of pure reason, but is one of practical judgment.

Such talk of judgment (or of intuition, moral insight, moral sensitivity, etc.) may raise the specter of practical judgments which are made *ad hoc* or otherwise arbitrarily and without rational constraints. In the next chapter, I shall attempt to allay this concern to some extent, by sketching a more positive account of practical reasoning. Expecting too much of practical reasoning may lead to skepticism with respect to it, but so may expecting too little.

CHAPTER VIII

BEYOND INTUITIONISM – A STEP

If the argument of the preceding chapter is accepted, then it appears that there can be no single fundamental practical principle, nor can there be a principle for the ordering of kinds of moral considerations. John Rawls has characterized as 'intuitionistic' those ethical theories which hold that there are a number of possibly conflicting 'first' principles, with no higher-level principle to determine priorities among them: 'we are to strike a balance by intuition'.[1] Even disregarding those views which involve moral skepticism and nihilism, it is by no means clear that the sole alternative to an appeal to exceptionless principles need be an appeal to unaided intuition; nor amongst those who are paradigmatically intuitionists, who emphasize the role of some sort of immediate apprehension of the moral quality of acts, need their intuitionism be based on the recognition of a conflict of principles. I shall say more on each of these points below.

For now, we may consider the picture of *prima facie* evaluative reasons, which must be 'weighed' against each other in the making of practical judgments, to represent the standard view of ethical intuitionism. To be sure, many philosophers who accept this much of the account, refuse to call themselves intuitionists. As I indicated above, there are other epistemological and metaphysical features associated with *intuitionism*, and perhaps taken as essential to it, which may account for this refusal. Be this as it may, it may be thought that the intuitionist account of *prima facie* moral reasons was decisively shown – once and for all – to be defective some time ago. The *locus classicus* of this supposed demonstration is P. F. Strawson's famous paper, 'Ethical Intuitionism'.[2] If one examines this paper, however, he will discover that the 'burial of inutitionism' which it (prematurely) announced is premised on the assumption that all valid reasoning is either deductive or inductive — in a narrow Humean sense of this latter term which requires the independent observability of both components of the process of inference, i.e., the data and the inferred entities or states of affairs. The untenability of this limitation is easily seen, since it rules out reasoning to (or from) those things which from the nature of the case (theoretical entities) or from the nature of their description (experiences of *others, past* events) are unobservable. The second class of cases provides much of the grist for the rather unproductive mills of traditional epistemology, where the limitation on reasoning which we are considering quickly leads to skepticism. Of late, we are told, we have been rescued from this dismal outcome by appeal to the Wittgensteinian notion of a *criterion*, or of the *criterial relation*, i.e., of a non-inductive defeasible evidential relation recognition of which P. M. S. Hacker has called 'Wittgenstein's main constructive contribution to contemporary philosophy'.[3] It seems to me (a) that the intuitionist account of moral reasoning clearly involves a non-inductive defeasible evidential relation, and thereby the notion of a *prima facie* reason anticipates the Wittgensteinian conception of a criterion — at least in the moral area, and (b) that a more satisfactory response to skeptical claims in epistemology than the criterial one is provided by a view which seeks to justify claims about other minds, etc., on the basis of their explanatory and predictive power.[4] Only, if the appeal to non-inductive, defeasible evidential relations *is* justified in the absence of something better, it can hardly be ruled out *a priori* in the area of practical reasoning.

On the view we are now considering, which involves *prima facie* evaluative reasons as the basis of practical judgment, the fundamental question would seem to be that of *weighing* these reasons. Even the question of whether or not a given fact is *relevant* to a particular practical judgment may be seen as subordinate to this question: it can be viewed as the question of whether or not the fact in question has *any* weight in our overall evaluation of the action. Now, as Rawls suggests, the ethical intuitionist holds that there is no overriding consideration to which each of the other considerations must be subordinate, and there is no independent principle for ordering the considerations in terms of their evaluative weight. But for this reason it may be thought that the intuitionists' account is, from a logical standpoint, incomplete, and that there *must* be some principle in terms of which we order moral reasons. Thus, D. H. Munro writes that

> The process of moral deliberation may appear to [a person] very much as Ross described it, as a more or less intuitive 'weighing' of different considerations until he finally decides that one or the other of the alternative courses of action is the right one. But such an account is clearly incomplete. The metaphor of 'weighing' presupposes some scale on which values are read off, some criteria (whether consciously realized or not) according to which the alternatives are compared.[5]

There are a number of things to be said about this passage, which clearly formulates a frequently made point. First, of course, is recognition that evaluative 'weighing' is a metaphorical notion which may not embody every feature of its literal counterpart. Moreover, even in the case of determining that one object is heavier than another by lifting each of them — perhaps the closest analogue of evaluative 'weighting' — should one say that one who makes such a judgment must have employed a criterion? Surely one can often make correct judgments of comparative weight by this method, but what *is* the *criterion* employed? Is something's *seeming* to be heavier than something else a criterion of its being heavier? If so, then the requirement of a criterion raises no problem for the ethical intuitionist. Here one must take quite seriously Wittgenstein's admonition that we not simply say that something must be the case, but that we look and see. If our making judgments presupposes our having criteria, we may well inquire what these criteria are. To be sure, if we are able to determine that an action is right (or, for that matter, that any characteristic is applicable to anything) then we must have a way of telling. And since a criterion may be characterized as a way of telling, talk of 'moral criteria' may simply reflect this trivial fact. But such talk may be, and, I submit, has been, seriously misleading. One could make a similar case for our having a 'moral faculty' (that we make moral judgments shows that we have the faculty of making them) but it would be similarly misleading. Speaking of 'moral criteria' is misleading because it suggests the existence of formulable principles under which the given case is to be subsumed (and, hence, a deductive model of practical justification). This suggestion may be reinforced by considerations pertaining to universalization which we discussed earlier, particularly the (trivial) point that if anything has a given property, then anything like it in all relevant respects will also have that property. As applied to moral reasoning, this becomes the truism that if a given action is right, then any action like it in all relevant respects will also be right. And this, too, may suggest an appeal to principles and to deductive justification. But, as I argued in the preceding chapter, if we succumb to such an appeal, we shall indeed have been misled by talk of 'criteria'.

There is within the tradition of ethical intuitionism a view which dispenses with the requirement of weighing conflicting reasons, but does so, as we shall see, at considerable cost for those con- concerned with the rational resolution of practical doubts or disagreements. The view in question is a view of practical reason- ing — or rather, of practical judgment — which has an excellent claim to the title (over which I have not the slightest wish to contend) of Ethical Intuitionism. It is the view whose most celebrated presentation occurs in H. A. Prichard's 'Does Moral

Philosophy Rest on a Mistake?'[6] On this account there is no such thing as practical *reasoning*, i.e., giving moral *reasons* in support of particular practical judgments. According to Prichard, all the *reasoning* is done in ascertaining and assembling the relevant facts in the case. Once this has been done there is no further reasoning; there is only 'moral thinking' whereby we come to 'appreciate' the obligatory character of a proposed act in light of the relevant facts. We may be misled into supposing that there are reasons supporting a practical judgment, reasons pertaining, e.g., to promise-keeping, or to consideration of consequences, by failure to realize that these are 'reasons' only insofar as the act is incompletely described; all these 'reasons' are simply part of the 'nature of the act'. Thus, when the 'nature of the act is completely stated' — and this statement is a task of general, not of moral reasoning — one does not, and indeed cannot, specify reasons to support the claim that the act ought (or ought not) to be performed; this practical judgment is based solely, at least for one who has attained a suitable level of moral development, on an 'appreciation' of the nature of the act.

Now it is obvious that Prichard assures the impossibility of there being evaluative reasons for an act by insisting that anything which normally would be accounted such a reason be incorporated into a complete description of the act itself. Although the distinction between an act and its antecedent conditions, or between an act and its consequences, is a function of the way in which 'the act' is described, there is little to recommend Prichard's account of a 'complete' statement of the nature of an act. For one thing, if any truth about an act is to count as part of such a complete statement; as Prichard's view suggests it must, and if moral thinking is to be based on such a statement, then clearly neither the statement nor the moral thinking based on it is possible: *all* truths about a given particular (whether action, object, or whatever) can never be stated. More importantly (since the foregoing difficulty is hardly peculiar to Prichard's account), this account seems to imply that a practically relevant antecedent conditions or consequence no matter how far removed temporally or spatially from what we should normally account a particular action, must form part of a complete description of the action. This sounds suspiciously like an arbitrary stipulation designed to support a particular theory.[7]

Normally, of course, we do distinguish between the description of an action and the statement of reasons — both evaluative and motivational — for or against its performance. It is important to preserve this distinction lest in (excessively) emphasizing the truly important role of sensitive judgment or appreciation of facts in the practical realm, we underemphasize or even deny the role of practical *reasoning*, and, thereby, the possibility of rational persuasion. The notion of rational persuasion has application to cases of judgment in which doubt or disagreement exists, and it is just in these cases that the sort of account of practical judgment given by Prichard appears to run into an immediate dead end.

To be sure, other forms of intuitionism, those that appeal to *prima facie* reasons, are beset by the same sort of difficulty. (And the reader hardly needs to be reminded that ethical theories based on general principles face rather obvious difficulties pertaining to the justification of those principles.) Neither one's weighing up of relevant reasons nor one's appreciation of all circumstances relevant for a complete description of an action need resolve one's own practical doubts or settle one's practical disagreements with another in a particular case. But a view which involves an appeal to *reasons* does provide some hope of going a step beyond the intuitionist impasse. There is, of course, no guarantee that a given attempt at the rational resolution of a practical doubt or disagreement will be successful. But this is a point which is by no means peculiar to the moral realm, although in other areas failure to attain a rationally based consensus is less likely to be seen as an argument for 'relativism'.[8]

But the question remains as to how we avoid the dead end of mere assertion and counter-assertion if we allow due weight to the role of sensitivity of judgment in determining both which considerations are relevant with respect to whether or not a particular action ought to be performed, and how much weight each of these (potentially conflicting) considerations has. The answer is that the same implicit generality which makes these considerations reasons also provides the basis for the *possibility* of rational persuasion *via* practical reasoning. Given the supervenient character of value characteristics there is, as we have seen, a kind of inconsistency involved in making different evaluations of cases which are without relevant factual differences. There is a strong temptation to try to incorporate relevant considerations into universal principles — a temptation to be resisted on theoretical, and, as will appear, on practical grounds.

In the normal run of cases, we need not deliberate at all on what we are to do; in the relatively few cases for which deliberation is necessary, the sort of process suggested by Prichard, that of bringing to mind the facts — including antecedents and consequences — of a particular action is usually sufficient for practical decision-making. But when this process is inadequate, as, when it fails to overcome disagreement as to what ought to be done, are we reduced to the level at which an exchange of charges of moral insensitivity is all that remains? It seems that this outcome can rationally be deferred, if not eliminated, and by a process very much like that of an appeal to principles — but without that appeal's attendant disadvantages. Still open in case a particular practical judgment is — in the absence of factual disagreement — disputed, is a kind of appeal to consistency, or to parity of reasoning.

Given agreement on the relevant facts of the case (a state of

affairs far less often realized than *moral* skeptics and *moral* relativists might lead one to believe, and practically never realized
in cases of major policy decisions of a political or economic sort,
or, say, in confrontations between representatives of different
nations, classes, etc.) we have *ipso facto* a common recognition
of everything which counts as an evaluative reason in the case,
although we may not have agreement *that* some particular fact
constitutes such a reason. If moral disagreement persists in the
face of factual agreement, an attempt at rational persuasion may
yet be made, not in terms of universal moral principles, which
would prove distracting, and ultimately futile, but in terms of
what might be called 'quasi-principles' — statements of evaluative
reasons having sufficient generality for the case at hand. The
process in question is one which is perfectly familiar in practice,
and one of which the reader probably needs only to be reminded.

Suppose that two persons disagree as to whether a certain
action, which involves the telling of a lie, ought to be performed.
We may assume that the two agree that the fact that the action
involves lying is a consideration against its being done, and,
further, that it is the only relevant negative consideration. The
proponent of the action will presumably cite some consideration
in favor of the action, perhaps in terms of expected consequences.
Now if the opponent of the action argues as a matter of principle
that one ought never to lie (and *a fortiori* that one ought not to
lie in the present case), then by overgeneralizing his claim he not
only greatly weakens it, but he also renders relevant to the case
in question other cases, real or imaginary, which are far removed
in character from the one at issue. Thus, the disputed case may
involve the issue of lying to spare another's feelings, whereas
the stated principle might involve cases, say, of lying to gain
for oneself the life savings of an elderly person. Obviously, the
justifiability of a case of the latter sort has little bearing on the
justifiability of one of the former sort, and to bring it in *via* an

appeal to principle (one, say, concerning lying in general) is to pay too high a price to avoid the appearance of defending a practical judgment in an *ad hoc* manner. This, admittedly, is rather an extreme sort of instance, since few would now, I think, categorically condemn lying in *every conceivable* situation, but analogous possibilities of bringing in irrelevant considerations and of unduly weakening one's case confront any attempt to justify a particular practical judgment by subsuming it under a general principle.

To avoid this Scylla of overgenerality without falling into the Charybdis of (*ad hoc*) overspecificity is a goal best attained for disputed practical judgments — if attainable at all — by what I call 'quasi-principles'. Quasi-principles permit the testing of a particular case by appeal to parallel cases — the principal function served by appeal to principles — without the overgeneralization involved in the appeal to principles. Since, as we have seen, practical judgments, being supervenient on factual judgments, are implicitly general, one mode of rational argument with respect to disputed practical judgments is to show (oneself or another) that one would give a different evaluation of an action for which one can ascertain no relevant factual difference. If one says of a particular action that it ought (not) to be performed, then one implies that any relevantly similar action ought (not) to be performed. If one notes some central feature (ϕ) in virtue of which the action ought (not) to be performed, and formulates a generalization to the effect that all actions which are ϕ, and are otherwise relevantly similar to the action in question, ought (not) to be performed then this generalization is a quasi-principle. (Presumably such a qualification about relevant similarities must in any case be understood as obtaining in any specification of a practical principle.) The quasi-principle is a completely universal statement, but its subject is specified not wholly in terms of some abstract characteristic of a particular (proposed) action — as it is in a genuine principle — but partly by reference to the action itself. So long as our concern is the assessment of the action, i.e., the making of a practical judgment, this is by no means a defect. Relevant abstract characteristics of the action are specified, and this specification may become exceedingly complex, but as long as the specification involves reference to the action being evaluated, the resulting generalization is still a quasi-principle. Thus, if one claims that a lie, or a lie told to one's mother to prevent her from worrying about her teen-age grandchild's use of marijuana, ought (not) to be told *under circumstances relevantly like those obtaining in the present case*, then that claim would be an instance of a quasi-principle, although without the underlined qualifying phrase, it would be a principle. (To be sure, in its more complex form, wherein it refers to a lie of a very complex sort, it is far less general than we normally expect moral principles to be.) If someone defends a particular practical judgment by specifying a reason in its favor, then he *may* be thought of as specifying a quasi-principle. Thus, we may not make an adequate criticism of his judgment by describing a case of an action having the characteristic specified in the reason, but for which the evaluation given is clearly inappropriate. But if we do describe such a case, then we are entitled to be told wherein it differs in morally relevant respects from the case in question. Since for most possible cases such relevant differences will be obvious, there will be no need for, or point to, their being mentioned, and cases with such differences would not serve as counter-instances to the quasi-principle, although they would to the corresponding principle. As in any other cases of finding counter-instances, luck and ingenuity play a central role, and failure to find one will not prove the quasi-principle and the particular judgment supported by it to be justified. On the other hand, to find a counter-instance, i.e., a case having no specifiable relevant difference from the one under consideration, but a case which nonetheless one would evaluate differently from the latter, is to find a kind of inconsistency in one's thinking; if, moreover, one is convinced that the evaluation involved in the proposed counter-instance is correct, one may then be persuaded – *rationally* persuaded – to alter his original practical judgment.

The appeal to quasi-principles is, of course, nothing more than the appeal to parity of reasoning. It enables us to bring to bear consideration of other cases when we attempt to evaluate a given action, and this, it seems to me, is just the advantage to be gained by appeal to principles. It does not, of course, enable us to dispense with 'intuitions'; nothing could do that, including basing our practical judgments on a single universal moral principle. Such a principle, if not completely arbitrary, would be the encapsulation of an indefinitely large number of particular judgments, and would have to be tested by reference to them.

Although I believe that an appeal to quasi-principles will do everything that an appeal to principles will do so far as the justification of particular practical judgments goes, I certainly do not wish to exaggerate the importance of such an appeal, especially since if we think of it as applying to practical judgments concerning which there are doubts or disagreements which are independent of factual uncertainties or disputes, its range of application may not be exceedingly large. Still, to be able, in effect, to look at a case from a different perspective can be extremely useful. This is so particularly if one's judgment of an action is unduly affected by the fact that the action has bearing on one's self, on one's friends, or, of course, on one's enemies. To see the action without these effects is to make possible a more disinterested, and thus a more rational, consideration of it. This is to claim for the appeal to quasi-principles the principal advantages attendant on an ideal observer theory[9] without the disadvantages of such a theory.

The appeal to quasi-principles is designed to take advantage of the central facts to which any reasonable form of intuitionism tacitly appeals, namely the fact that we are all trained, and re-markably successful, moral evaluators. Our evaluative ability is manifested in our constant, unhesitating making of practical judgments on which (nearly) all agree. Those of a naturalist-empiricist temper have tended to disparage talk of 'intuitionism', partly because it seemed to appeal to some sort of very mysterious faculty. But there need be nothing mysterious about our ability as evaluators — presumably it has a perfectly straightforward physiological/socio-psychological explanation. Now we all rec-ognize that simple application of this ability ('appeal to intuition') sometimes fails us in that it does not resolve all our practical doubts or disagreements. In such cases, appeal to quasi-principles is designed to do what appeal to principles is supposed to do, namely, to put the case in question in with a suitable comparison class with the hope of aiding our intuitions. A dialogue involving the presentation of putatively parallel cases may help the partici-pants to get clearer about their own views as to what constitutes a relevant consideration, even if it does not dispel disagreement.

I realize that these comments on practical reasoning are overly abstract and extremely incomplete; thus, I have left the task of providing examples almost entirely to the reader. (These failings are to be excused only marginally on the ground that my comments are expressly designed as *prolegomena*.) Moreover, while emphasizing the role of relevantly similar cases in the evaluation of a given practical judgment, I have said nothing, e.g., about consideration of the relative value of genuinely possible alternative courses of action, obviously a point of the greatest importance in determining whether or not a given action ought to be performed.

However incomplete and otherwise unsatisfactory these re-marks may be, I think they point in a useful direction for anyone concerned with the rational resolution of practical doubts or disagreements. A rational individual must recognize the limits

on the role of reason in *persuasion* in any area, but especially
in one where feelings and attitudes tend to be centrally involved.
And as anyone who has participated in or observed theoretical
debate can attest, these factors can become involved virtually
anywhere. But one must not underestimate the possible role of
reason either (and suppose that feelings and attitudes are all that
really matter), especially in the realm of practical judgment.
Continual, or even occasional, testing of one's practical judgments
by appeal to one's quasi-principles, with suitable adjustments of
the judgments — or of the putative principles, will help one to
eliminate irrationality in one's moral beliefs, and will yield, at the
ideal limit, a complete consistency in one's practical judgments.
While for others we might prefer an *alteration* of particular moral
judgments to an increase in their consistency, we cannot reasonably have a similar preference in our own case. If all our moral
beliefs were rendered clear and consistent there could be no
(external) standard against which *we* could judge them. To be
sure, neither clarity nor consistency can guarantee wisdom, truth,
or even inter-subjective agreement. So we may be tempted to say
that clarity and consistency are 'not enough'. Not only, however,
is each infinitely preferable to its obvious alternative, but in the
realm of practical judgment they — together, of course with
relevant factual knowledge — are the basis for the best that any
individual may hope to attain.

CHAPTER IX

"TO FORGIVE ALL . . . "

> "It's no sin to be poor − but it might as well be."
> — Abe Martin

We return in this chapter to the question of the conditions under which we are justified in holding persons obligable for their actions. In light of what has been said in the preceding two chapters, it should obviously not be expected that I shall attempt to propound a general formula in terms of which to answer this question. Rather, I shall merely suggest some of the considerations that must be weighed in making reasonable judgments of obligability and, more generally, in justifying the practice of making such judgments. Since reference to the overall causal structure of the universe plays no role in deciding questions of obligability in a particular case, this is a further indication of the independence of the question of obligability from that of determinism/indeterminism. Still so strong is the seductive power of the pictures associated with these exotic metaphysical doctrines that our fidelity to our homely, everyday notion of obligability may be weakened − at least while we are under the spell of these pictures. So I shall say more in opposition to the *general* rejection of obligability, which, as I have argued, is based on the acceptance of an inadequate *principle* of non-obligability. I have suggested that this general rejection is paradoxical, or, at least highly infelicitous. But, in addition, the practice of holding persons obligable has, at the practical level, much to recommend it beyond the avoidance of conceptual difficulty.

It is our practice to hold persons responsible for their actions in the absence of excusing conditions and, more generally, to hold persons obligable for them in the absence of absolving conditions. This general practice is capable of pragmatic defense or justification of a rather obvious sort to be discussed below. Whether, in a particular case, the presumption of obligability is overcome, must be determined by factors operative in that case. Given this truism, we find that sometimes individuals are obligable and sometimes they are not. The stability of this view, despite its boring obviousness, is threatened by generalization over some of those considerations which not infrequently constitute absolving conditions; this generalization yields the OES supposition. This supposition, as a practical *principle* states that non-substitutability is a general absolving condition, or, in other words, that if there are sufficient conditions for an action traceable to factors outside the agent's control, then the action (and its agent) are not obligable. From this principle we can quickly infer the exciting conclusion that no one is ever really obligable.

I do not intend to review here what I believe to be wrong with this argument. I am, moreover, even willing to allow that the phrase " 'ought' implies 'can' " has been repeated so frequently among philosophers that a sense of 'obligability' or of 'responsibility' — denoting 'real' or 'absolute' obligability or responsibility — may have developed which is such that these terms have no possible application. (Though why, once this implication is clear, anyone should still be interested in these notions, is hard to see.) Still, I must insist on two points. First, if we allow, for the sake of argument, that no one is ever *really* obligable, nonetheless we may still distinguish between cases in which we are justified in *holding* a person 'obligable', i.e., cases in which we are justified in praising or blaming a given individual for his action, and other cases, in which we are not. This distinction, moreover, is of fundamental practical importance. Second, if, in a given case, someone (e.g., Clarence Darrow, in defense of a client) gives an argument using abstract notions of 'heredity' and 'environment' to show an agent's non-obligability in that case, but if the argument is sufficiently general to apply to *anyone*, then this argument, being, in effect, simply an instance of the general abstract argument against obligability, has no tendency to show that the agent is not justifiably to be praised, blamed, rewarded, or punished under applicable and acceptable moral or legal standards.

The case for general non-obligability, or for non-obligability in a particular case supported only by the sort of argument ("the agent is the victim, or product, of his genetic make-up, and environmental factors") which would or will support a general claim of non-obligability, is commonly made when we are concerned with excusing conditions — rather than with absolving conditions generally — and has its greatest appeal when we think of it as applying to persons who, either individually or as members of groups, are somehow victimized, oppressed, or disadvantaged. But, of course, insofar as the argument is one which supports universal non-obligability, it as well rules out deserved praise for the noblest of persons, as it rules out blame for the cruelest. ("After all, the noble person is merely fortunate to have tendencies — whether learned or inherited — to act in such and such ways.") Moreover, such an argument obviously applies as well to the perpetrators of horrendous crimes as to their victims. From the point of view in question, 'Goose-step a mile in my jack-boots' is as reasonable an admonition as 'Walk a mile in my mocassins'. These considerations are designed to remind the reader — surely not to argue, since the point does not appear to require argument — that general claims of non-obligability, even when tacitly relying on our feelings of compassion, may miss the whole point of our practice of holding persons obligable, and may do so, moreover, in a manner which is more patronizing than it is compassionate. Charity may be the greatest of the virtues, but our misguided efforts to be charitable to one individual may harm not only his victims but the person himself. The very notion of being a person is closely tied to that of being obligable: genuinely to see another being − or oneself − as a person is to see that being as the bearer of responsibility. To deny obligability to an individual (or to members of a group) is to deny the individual(s) complete personhood; it is to attribute to the individual(s) in question at most the nature of an animal or of a child. If to understand all *were* to forgive all, then, even more obviously, to forgive all would be to *forgive* nothing. To excuse generally on the basis of a supposed universal excusing condition is to empty the notion of excuse of any useful function; to excuse selectively on such a basis, i.e., on the basis of considerations which have universal application, is not only unfair as a form of special pleading, it is, equally importantly, an affront to the dignity of those so excused. I suggested earlier that claims of universal non-obligability are paradoxical; now I suggest that the sort of abstract arguments used to support these claims lead to conclusions which are morally unacceptable as well.

By now it is becoming obvious that, with all due respect to the opinions of C. D. Broad as well as to those of the host of hard determinists, a general defense of the notion of obligability may not only be otiose but it may become embarrassingly preachy. Broad's view cuts deeper than does that of the hard determinists, since it shows that given a supplemental assumption which it shares with these determinists (the OES supposition) obligability is ruled out regardless of the truth or falsity of determinism.[1] Broad's analysis thereby provides much of the basis for − although it fails to recognize − a *reductio ad absurdum* of the OES supposition. Without this supposition, the practical problem of free will should dissolve.

Still, I recognize that the (highly abstract) argument against the compatibility of obligability and determinism casts a spell which it is hard to break, possibly because of imagery which it arouses. And, on this point, it is not difficult to contrast a *picture* of a world in which every event, including human actions, is an element in a causal chain going back in time indefinitely, so that whatever happens is causally necessitated by antecedent events, with a *picture* in which certain events, namely (some) human actions, are elements in causal chains going back only to the agents. But, of course, the possibility of these contrasting *pictures* does nothing to show the tenability or even the coherence of the libertarian theory which the latter image may suggest. Here I have in mind particularly the theory of (immanent) agent-causation which I discussed in Chapter III above. There are other pictures of a deterministic world, such as that of James' 'block-universe' or of Whitehead's world in which 'the molecules blindly run', which suggest the total ineffectiveness of all human action, and which thereby render the claims of determinism unpalatable. Despite these pictures, determinism as such does not render our actions ineffective, although the world — whether or not events in it fall completely under natural laws — may *be* unpalatable.[2] In any event, without speculating further as to why, we may simply note that *determinism* is thought to pose a special problem for human obligability. Now I have insisted repeatedly — indeed, I fear repetitiously — that the appearance of incompatibility between determinism and obligability arises principally from a failure to raise the same sort of questions of compatibility with respect to indeterminism and obligability that we raise with respect to determinism and obligability. But in addition to such considerations which are designed to show the inconclusive character of incompatibility claims, we may take a more direct approach and look at cases in which the attribution of obligability seems justified, with a view to showing that the existence of such cases is not incompatible with the assumption of the truth of determinism. Restricting this discussion to the question of the compatibility of obligability and determinism is designed merely as a simplifying assumption; it is intended neither to assert the truth of determinism nor to suggest anything about the compatibility or the incompatibility of indeterminism and obligability.

Assuming then, merely for the sake of argument, the truth of determinism, we may characterize that doctrine roughly, but well enough for the incompatibilist's intended purposes, as that which maintains that for every event e, there is some other (event or) set of events which occur antecedently to or simultaneously with e, and whose occurrence constitutes a sufficient condition for the occurrence of e. Since 'standing conditions' will obviously form part of the sufficient condition of events, as, e.g., the presence of oxygen in a room at time t_1 is part of the sufficient condition of the conflagration in the room beginning at t_1, the use of 'event' here should be understood in an extended sense in which it may be applied to anything dateable. This formulation of the deterministic position is designed to be neither precise nor generally useful — it is intended merely as a basis for raising the incompatibilist's concerns. It should serve to arouse this *Angst* by assuring that on its terms there is an obvious sense in which no actual event, and *a fortiori* no actual human action, could have failed to occur, since if the sufficient conditions of an event occur or exist, the event occurs. And if an action cannot but occur, then its agent — in the familiar phrase — 'cannot (could not) do otherwise' than perform (have performed) it.

On the assumption of determinism, then, how is the practice of holding persons obligable to be justified? To raise the question in this way is not to suggest that our practice with respect to obligability is completely defined and totally agreed upon by 'us', or that to the extent to which it is accepted it is, in all details, acceptable. Indeed, all that is required is that there should be *some* justified practice of holding persons responsible which is compatible with determinism. Only, one may assume that existing societies have managed, by a process of experimental sifting to retain, in general, those practices which are conducive to the preservation of the societies and to the relative well-being of at least a substantial number of their members. To justify a practice, one provides a pragmatic justification for it. I intend that statement as analytic. But an important part of a pragmatic justification is that which is ordinarily so-called, namely, justification of an action or set of actions in terms of the consequences of the performance of the action(s). Such consequentialist considerations form an important part of any reasonable attempt to justify the practice of ascribing obligability.

Now it is imperative to face up squarely to the fact that determinism implies that in an obvious sense, as we have seen, no one could have acted otherwise than he in fact did, and to reconcile this fact with ascribing obligability to agents. (As usual, it is helpful to remind oneself that though *in*determinism has no implication of the causal inevitability of particular events, this fact alone, for reasons which should by now be familiar, has precisely *no* tendency to show that on the assumption of indeterminism an agent could have *done* something other than what he did.) It is especially important to recognize this (non--substitutability) implication of determinism in order to suggest to soft determinists why it is that their claim that there are *other* uses of 'could have done otherwise' than the one in question, seems to their opponents a fact which is not at all, or is at best peripherally, relevant to the free will problem. I shall not here comment any further on the use of 'could have done otherwise' to signify the mere absence of an absolving condition. But the oft-discussed hypothetical analysis of that expression — while in several ways inadequate, as I have argued above — does suggest a consideration of importance for our present purposes. An adequate reminder of the inadequacy of any attempt to provide a hypothetical analysis of 'X could have done otherwise', i.e.

one equating that expression with 'X would have done otherwise if he had so desired (or tried, or whatever)' is provided by consideration of an individual acting under a compulsive desire, or while his will is subject to that of another. In such cases we should *not* say that the individual could have acted otherwise, even though it is true that *if* he had desired or tried, he would have acted otherwise, since he could not desire or try to act otherwise.

But, as I have indicated, the question of whether or not a person would have acted otherwise if he had been suitably motivated, is relevant to our present inquiry, in that an affirmative answer to that question, i.e., the question of hypothetical substitutability, appears to represent a necessary condition of any event's being a genuine action. Unfortunately for the neatness of this investigation, hypothetical substitutability nonetheless does not appear to be either a necessary or a sufficient condition of obligability. The first point is not paradoxical: even if hypothetical substitutability is a necessary condition of something's being an action, it need not be a necessary condition of obligability since obligability is defined for omissions and failures to act as well as for (positive) actions. Thus, an individual may not be absolved of obligability for failing to act (where this failure involves, say, the non-fulfillment of an obligation) even if performing the act is not something he could do if he so desired. For the individual may have unjustifiably put himself in a position where he is not able to perform the action (i.e., where he cannot but fail to perform the action) even if he desires to do so. (Recall, e.g., the case of the individual who has gambled away the money he had promised to repay.)

I do not wish to make terribly much of the claim that hypothetical substitutability is not a necessary condition of obligability, especially since to this claim it may be objected that one is obligable for a failure to act which is not directly within one's power to avoid, only if this lack of power results predictably from an earlier action or omission which was both hypothetically substitutable and obligable. Thus, on this objection, hypothetical substitutability is, at least indirectly, a necessary condition of obligability. Although this point may be granted, two further points should be kept in mind. The first is that even if hypothetical substitutability is a necessary condition of obligability, the judgment that it is − in contrast to the judgment that hypothetical substitutability is a necessary condition of something's being an action − is an evaluative one. If we refuse to consider a person obligable for that which is not hypothetically substitutable, it is because we judge that it would be pointless, or unfair, or immoral to do so. On the other hand, if we refuse to consider something not hypothetically substitutable an action, even though it be ascribed, using the active voice, to an agent (Mary fell, or grew; John died, or felt pain, e.g.), it is because we judge it to lack a defining characteristic of an *action*. Clearly, this distinction will be recognized only by one who does not construe 'obligable' as a straight-forwardly descriptive term. That it ought not to be so construed is seen in the fact that whether or not a given condition *absolves* of obligability is a matter for evaluative judgment (as to whether, e.g., a person's ignorance was *culpable*, or whether someone *ought* to have given in to threats). The more important point has to do with the question of how this relationship between hypothetical substitutability and obligability is supposed to help show the compatibility of obligability and determinism, given the latter's implicit categorical non-substitutability. To be sure, hypothetical substitutability is *compatible with* categorical non-substitutability ('X would have ϕ'd if he had wanted to' is compatible with 'X couldn't want to ϕ' − cf. 'pigs would fly if they had wings'.) But it is only if hypothetical substitutability were a *sufficient* condition for obligability that our question would be directly answered.

And, of course, hypothetical substitutability is not a sufficient condition of obligability. For one may be absolved of obligability even if his action is one which he could have avoided had he so desired, provided only that it would have been unjustifiable to expect him to have, and to act on, the alternative desire. (This is just the sort of case in which we use the expression 'he couldn't have done otherwise' simply to express a judgment of non-obligability, as in the case of the bank teller who gives up money to an armed robber.) More generally, if, as appears, hypothetical substitutability is a necessary condition of one's genuinely *acting*, then any case in which there exists an absolving condition of any sort, whether it is based on compulsion, ignorance, provocation, mistake, or whatever, is a case in which hypothetical substitutability is not a sufficient condition of obligability.

Nonetheless, hypothetical substitutability is a fundamental consideration in any serious attempt to show the compatibility of determinism and obligability. As I have suggested above, the apparent incompatibility of the two is based on an overgeneralization which fails to distinguish obligable from non-obligable actions. As suggested in the previous chapter, what must be done to combat an excessively general evaluative claim is to indicate practically relevant differences between cases. It is reference to an agent's reasons for acting[3] which, I suggest, provides the basis for distinguishing within a deterministic framework between obligable and non-obligable actions. And the justification for the claim that these differences are relevant rests in large measure on points related to the notion of hypothetical substitutability, *viz.*, to the dependence of the action on the agent's desires and to certain ways in which the desires can be restrained or overcome.

Let us proceed by considering two kinds of cases from which generalizations about obligability may be drawn. The first involve an absence of hypothetical substitutability, and are not genuinely a person's *actions*. Such cases would be ones, e.g., in which a person is washed overboard by a huge wave, or thrown overboard by another person. One who supposes determinism incompatible with obligability (an incompatibilist) may do so because he supposes that determinism renders such cases, and especially the former, paradigms of human behavior, ruling out the possibility of genuine human actions, and, *a fortiori* that of obligable actions. He supposes that determinism makes these cases standard, because he takes it that the existence of sufficient causal conditions for the occurrence is the feature in virtue of which the occurrence is not an (obligable) action. And since, on the determinist view, this feature characterizes *every* event, the incompatibilist may take it that on this view, there are no genuine actions, and that the 'agent' is simply the helpless victim of causal factors outside his control.

The compatibilist will naturally counter with the observation that the cases suggested, not being cases of human action, can hardly be *standard* cases of human action, much less of obligable human action. (Incidentally, I need not remind the reader that a person is not automatically absolved of obligability for what is described as 'being washed overboard': he may, e.g., thoughtlessly, or even deliberately − in order, say, to commit suicide − put himself in a position during a storm where he is virtually certain to be swept into the sea. This is obviously not the sort of case being imagined.) He will observe further that standard cases of human action are distinguished by the fact that among their causes are desires, pro-attitudes, of the agent, and, moreover, that a person who performs an action because he wants to do so is hardly to be described as a 'victim' of circumstances.

Now it appears that it is from this last observation that some of the compatibilist's preoccupation with the role of hypothetical substitutability arises. For surely the compatibilist's concern for the fact that an agent would have acted differently if he had wanted to is not to be explained by the former's joy over disasters averted or sadness over opportunities missed. Rather, this concern arises because hypothetical substitutability is indicative of the causal efficacy of the agent's desires in the action which he in fact performed: this efficacy is manifested by the fact that had they been different, the action performed would have been different. Indeed, we normally take hypothetical substitutability as a sufficient condition of an action's resulting from an agent's desire because of the difficulties involved in obtaining independent evidence of the occurrence of such (desiring) states or dispositions.

While hypothetical substitutability may be a necessary condition of a bodily movement's being an action, it does not appear to be a sufficient condition. And the sorts of case that illustrate this fact serve to raise considerations that may seem to reinstate the difficulties that talk of hypothetical substitutability was designed to remove. Suppose first − what is for now, at least, a kind of science-fiction possibility − that a mad scientist were able to control in the smallest detail the brain states of another person by means of the transmission of mysterious rays. Now if the scientist were to affect the behavior of the other not by directly triggering muscle-contractions and hence bodily movements, but by causing certain desires to act and ruling out alternative desires, the resulting behavior, though it might appear, both to the agent and to others, to be an action of the agent's, would in fact not be such, even though it might be true that if the agent had desired to act differently, he would have. We should attribute the *action* (as opposed to the movement) not to the scientist's *patient*, but to the scientist. Even, however, if we were at all times the unknowing victims of such a mad scientist, discovering this fact, while shattering to our self-esteem, would be by no means destructive of the notions of action and of agency − it would merely transfer the locus of their applicability.

But suppose that the same results − alterative of our brain states so that we have certain desires and no conflicting ones − were brought about not as the result of personal agency, but as the result of natural forces. Would this, from the point of view of the individual whose behavior results from the desire, be relevantly different from the case in which the desire is brought about by the omega rays of the mad scientist? In this case, too, desires are causally efficacious, and hypothetical substitutability of the individual's action — or 'action'[4] — obtains. But here, it seems, we cannot just transfer the locus of agency — we leave no room for the applicability of the concept of action at all. And isn't this just what determinism leads us to? (As always, before being carried away by arguments or claims against determinism, one is well advised to ask how the assumption of *in*determinism provides a way out of the difficulty.)

This question may be intended as a rhetorical one, but it turns out to be a genuine question with a negative answer. For, though the situations imagined first with and then without the mad scientist do indeed share an important feature with cases of action as they would be correctly described on the assumption of determinism, they differ in one essential respect, as can be seen by consideration of any standard case of human actions. Actions resemble the cases imagined in that the desires for their occurrence have causes. This is obviously a point required on the assumption of determinism, but it is not one which should appear threatening to the existence of actions, or, indeed, of free actions, on *any* hypothesis concerning the causal structure of the universe. For surely it is a familiar fact that under suitable circumstances perceptual experience will trigger certain desires (whatever the neuro-physiological mechanisms involved may be). The sight and smell of food, e.g., may cause a desire to eat, if one is hungry, and indeed may even cause a very strong desire to eat the very food which one has seen and smelled. The strength and direction of the desire, whether brought about by the manipulation of one's nervous system by the mad scientist, or by familiar 'natural' causes may be the same and in any event the desire will be caused.

What distinguishes the two sorts of cases is that in the former, as described, the possible efficacy of alternative desires is ruled out. In the case of a normal human being there exist all sorts of standing motivational factors, some of which may be classified as prudential, others as moral, still others as impersonal (aesthetic, scientific, e.g.), etc. Now in the mad scientist case, all these factors are simply set aside in favor of a single overpowering desire. Thus, e.g., as the situation is imagined, a person whose desire to eat the apple in front of him will straightway do so, unless, of course, he is physically restrained. Nothing less will prevent him from eating the apple. In particular, no reasons, i.e. motives effected by beliefs will be effectual. Thus, his motivation strictly controlled by the mad scientist, our victim will not be deterred from eating the apple by his recognition that he is taking it from a hungry child, or even by his recognition that the apple is poisoned.

We may contrast this case with one in which a person's eating an apple is an action — obviously the normal case. In this case, too, the agent wants to eat the apple, and his desire has causes. But the agent is not the 'slave of this desire', i.e., other considerations may affect his decision to eat the apple or to refrain from eating it. Some, e.g., the agent's belief that eating the apple will be good for his health or for the economy, will reinforce his desire; others, such as those mentioned above, will count against, and almost certainly defeat, the desire. Thus, although hypothetical substitutability is not strictly a sufficient condition for some behavior's being a bit of action, still since in standard cases, a desire, which is a reason for action, operates in the context of a number of other reasons, some of which may support and others oppose the desire, and since in actual cases there seems no reason to suppose that the appearance of efficacy of reasons on decisions to act is deceptive, we may conclude that for all practical purposes hypothetical substitutability is a sufficient condition for the existence of actions, and hence that the assumption of determinism, even if it appears to be a threat to obligability, is compatible with the existence of actions. To be sure, some bits of behavior which we may tend to classify as actions and which are hypothetically substitutable may not be *actions* if their motivating force is such that it cannot be overridden by other considerations. Perhaps some 'acts of passion' are of this sort. But this kind of case must be distinguished from that in which the strength of the motivation is such as to make its being overridden *very difficult* for the agent — this seems to be the case at least with respect to any given action attributed to such 'manias' as kleptomania, pyromania, etc. Cases of this latter sort seem best classified as actions, with the recognition, of course, that their peculiar motivations provide the basis for extenuation or, perhaps of absolution from obligability. In any case, if even only a few bits of hypothetically substitutable behavior fall outside the range of the compulsive, the notion of action will have application. And the evidence supports the claim that most of such behavior constitutes action.

This consideration, even if accepted, will hardly placate the incompatibilist. He will surely maintain that even if actions are distinguishable on the determinist view from other behavior, still on that view, in terms of which no event could have happened other than it did, the distinction is of no significance. For, since alternatives *desires* (causally) could not have occurred, the supposition of hypothetical substitutability can represent at best idle speculation without any practical relevance. It is a matter of some importance, I think, to feel the force of the incompatibilist's objections (always bearing in mind the question of how an indeterminist alternative — here, say, of an uncaused desire suddenly becoming part of the agent's motivational repertoire — is supposed to render the agent obligable), and even to feel puzzled by them. I mention this point because I think that many soft determinists think that they answer the incompatibilist's objections by differentiating causation from compulsion, or by identifying substitutability with hypothetical substitutability, or by suggesting that a different notion of causation is used in 'the sciences of man as man'.[5] Each of these suggestions points out something of importance, but all fail adequately to deal with the incompatibilist's objection that if determinism is true, and that every event falls under a causal law or that there is an independent sufficient condition for every happening, then nothing can happen other than it does. The compatibilist must face up to that implication of determinism (although, to repeat, he need not suppose that determinism is true; i.e., a compatibilist need not be a soft *determinist*).

Every dateable state of affairs or change of state is, then, assumed to be a link in a causal chain, or, better, an element in a causal net. Now assuming further that we can distinguish a class of events which we call human actions, we may be troubled as to why the agents of these actions should be held obligable for them. We have seen in more than sufficient detail, I fear, why non-substitutability is not sufficient as an absolving condition. But we can perhaps say something a bit more positive as to what distinguishes obligable actions and as to why these distinctions are relevant. Not surprisingly, the considerations are quite familiar, although their delineation is not without its difficulties.

If we are to justify an instance (or a practice) of holding a person (or persons) obligable, the instance or practice must accomplish or contribute to something which we consider desirable. This poor truism is at the heart of our justificatory task. To be sure, in order to have a point, the attribution of obligability must first make sense. Thus there is no point, because there is no sense, in holding a stone obligable for hurting someone — although if there were a point to so doing we might have defined 'obligable' so as to make its applicability to inanimate objects intelligible. This last point must be handled with caution, as Campbell's examples of children and non-human animals mentioned in Chapter III above remind us. Evidently, the efficacy of rewards or punishments, or of positive or negative reinforcement of behavior depends on the ability of individuals to initiate actions (the imposition of suitable reinforcements will serve to encourage or to discourage the initiation of similar behavior in the future); and this ability other animals share with adult humans. But possession of this ability is not sufficient for agency of the sort required for obligability. Such agency requires the possibility of choice, the possibility of considering and weighing the desirability of alternative courses of action in a given situation. This possibility seems restricted to beings with the sort of conceptual-linguistic capabilities found, in our experience, only in adult humans.

I realize that such talk of 'choice' must appear questionable to the incompatibilist; indeed it lies at the heart of his objections to determinism. The reason for this is obvious enough: choice involves the genuine possibility of a number of actions; determinism implies that whatever action is performed could not but have been performed. But by now it should be clear that any incompatibility in these two claims is apparent only. The latter claim, whatever may be *suggested* by its formulation, involves only the existence of sufficient conditions for the occurrence of the action (and sufficient conditions for these . . .), while the fact that an agent weighs the desirability of a number of actions which lie within the range of his abilities and opportunities surely does nothing to show that there are not sufficient conditions for that action which he is fact decides to perform. (Indeed, the fact that it occurs demonstrates that for it, and for none of its alternatives, sufficient conditions do exist.)

Still, if the notion of obligability may, consistently with the assumption of determinism, have application, when and why are we justified in attributing it to agents? In attempting to answer this question, we must beware of the supposition that a single kind of consideration will suffice. Traditionally, compatibilists have been soft determinists who have tended to base their justification of the ascription of responsibility entirely on utilitarian or consequentialist grounds. Surely, utilitarian considerations are important in trying to justify claims of obligability, but we must expect other sorts of considerations, especially those of justice, to be relevant to such attempts. Thus we generally consider it unjustified, because unjust, to hold anyone obligable for an action he has not performed despite the utility which might be served by so doing. (I am assuming that the use of 'obligable' is construed — or stretched — so that this case is not ruled out analytically.)

Now it strikes me, as I have suggested, that in the most familiar compatibilist tradition — that associated with such names as Hume, Mill, Schlick, and Smart, e.g. — the justification of the practice of holding individuals obligable has been too narrowly tied to consequentialist considerations. This is unfortunate in several ways. First, as we have noted, if the justification of holding individuals obligable consists of the fact that use of rewards and punishments will serve to modify behavior in socially desirable ways, then the notion of obligability will be applicable not only to small children but to animals far down the evolutionary scale. And it is a bit counter-intuitive to ascribe moral responsibility not only to children, but to dogs, rats, and earthworms. One could suggest that the differences with respect to obligability as we move up or down the scale are merely ones of degree. While this suggestion helps us keep in mind that there is no sharp line to be drawn for the determination of the stage at which a human being becomes a responsible person, it seems clear that our notion of moral responsibility simply does not correspond with that of the effectiveness of blame or punishment. Perhaps the suggestion is that it *should*; but insofar as the suggestion rests on nothing more than a clear line of demarcation for obligability, it is no more persuasive than the claim, say, that there is no real difference between (those paradigms of difference) black and white or day and night. As a matter of fact, moreover, there are good reasons − indeed good reasons of largely a consequentialist sort − for holding obligable only those individuals whose behavior is capable of being influenced by the abstract presentation of reasons (i.e., adult human beings).

A more serious defect in a purely consequentialist defense of the attribution of obligability has also been alluded to earlier. This defect involves classes of cases in which we should judge that, in general, attribution of obligability would be unfair or undeserved, even though the consequences of this attribution would be useful. One such class of cases would be that in which members of a criminal wrong-doer's family or other group to which the criminal belongs are punished (or 'punished') for the criminal's transgressions. This, of course, is a practice which is not unknown historically, but is one which must challenge our sense of justice, even if, say, it is effective in lowering the crime rate. To be sure, holding a group obligable for a member's actions may be justified − even if not just − in extreme circumstances, as when, for example, penalizing the group can be shown to be the only effective way of reducing a crime rate which threatens a society's very existence. But if consideration of consequences, as opposed, say, to consideration of the justice of our procedures, were the *sole* consideration in determining the justifiability of a practice, then holding other persons obligable for a criminal's actions might be justified even if the practice were only *marginally* successful in lowering the rate of crime.

It might be stated as an objection to the foregoing example that the persons penalized in the extreme case were not really obligable: they had not performed or failed to perform any actions which rendered them blameworthy, nor had they manifested any relevant anti-social character traits. But it should be clear that this fact is not an objection to my claim that a consequentialist account in terms of which obligability is a function of the effectiveness of sanctions in promoting socially approved and preventing socially disapproved modes of behavior is inadequate; rather, if the effectiveness of sanctions applied to individuals does not even show those individuals to be obligable, then this fact *supports* my claim. As remarked above, there are historical precedents for considering one responsible for actions of other members of one's tribe, family, or other social group. Perhaps these precedents rest on a more organic, less individualistic conception of an agent than the one we now have. In any event, we can conceive of the (re-)institution of the practice of holding (and considering) individuals fully obligable for the actions of members of groups to which they belong. (Even now we see nothing conceptually odd about persons' being *proud* or *ashamed* of actions performed by members of their families, or of their communities, or even of their clubs, universities, nations, or races.) But whether or not we suppose that there are conceptual objections to counting individuals *obligable* for the actions of others (where those others are not under the authority of those accounted obligable), we must surely find moral objections to so doing: the practice of *proxy-punishment*, i.e., of penalizing an individual for the infractions of, say, a fugitive member of that person's family, must strike us as quite unjust, and to be avoided except in the most extreme circumstances regardless of how socially useful the practice may be discovered to be.

We may note, incidentally, that proxy-punishment — whether or not one thinks it is 'really' a form of *punishment* — could be instituted (for certain classes of cases) as a social practice. In this respect it differs from cases standardly urged against consequentialist or utilitarian theories, e.g., cases of punishing innocent persons, say, to counter a dangerous level of social hysteria due to an unsolved series of crimes. For such cases, it is essential that the status of the victim be falsely represented to the public. Thus, there could not be a publicly known institutionalized practice of punishing innocent scapegoats. But if this fact is used by the con-sequentialist to respond to this sort of objection to his theory, it is a response which is not available in the case of proxy-punishment.

One further point about the envisaged practice of proxy-pun-ishment: there are cases in which persons are obligable for the actions of others (e.g., parents for certain activities of their minor children), and if they are punished for the actions of these others for which they are responsible, this does *not* constitute what I am calling proxy-punishment. The latter practice involves applying penalties to an individual in whom a malefactor has an interest, in order to cause the latter to alter his behavior (to give himself up to the authorities, or to refrain from similar behavior in the future, e.g.). The individual penalized need not be thought of as in any way obligable; what is involved is the attempt to influence the behavior of the responsible person by applying penalties to one whom the latter is concerned about. Quite simply, proxy-punishment is a form of institutionalized blackmail; this is why it offends our moral sensibilities even when or if it serves to maximize social utility.

What I have called proxy-punishment represents but one of innumerable sorts of cases in which our concern for an intrinsic value such as that of justice *may* run counter, in the evaluation of a proposed or actual practice, to considerations of social utility. Many of these cases may not raise questions concerning the obli-gability of agents to be rewarded or punished, but, nonetheless, they help to show that consideration of consequences cannot reasonably be thought of as the sole basis for the evaluation of practices. Thus, practices involving censorship or wiretapping, or other infringements on liberties or invasions of privacy, *may* have greater social utility than do alternative practices. Still, given the intrinsically undesirable character of interfering with the civil liberties of our fellow citizens – and the interferences envisaged are *components*, not *consequences* – it is by no means a foregone conclusion that those practices ought to be instituted. (Nor I may add, is it a *totally* foregone conclusion that they should not be instituted in *any* case.)

One natural response of the consequentialist to these claims deserves attention. It is that concern for such supposedly intrinsic values as justice, liberty, honesty, etc., is rational only because of the desirable consequences of actions or of practices embodying these characteristics. Insofar as this claim is thought to be justified by the fact that in suitable circumstances consequential factors may outweigh the consideration of such values, the premise simply fails to support the conclusion. But I suspect that something more underlies the consequentialist's claim, namely a theory as to the basis for our original acceptance of non-consequentialist values. The theory is that these values are accepted in the first instance because their implementation has good consequences. Thus, the practices of truth-telling, promise-keeping, respect for privacy, etc., prove to have social utility, and it this fact which justifies their acceptance. But, the (implicit) argument continues, we develop a kind of fixation on these values, forgetting why we hold them, just as, say, the miser develops a fixation on intrinsically valueless paper money. These values, then, are not truly intrinsic: as rational individuals we accept them only insofar as they contribute to some good consequence. (And the argument is bolstered by consideration of cases in which expectation of extremely bad consequences would lead us justifiably, say, to lying or to breaking a promise.)

Now even waiving all consideration of the truth or falsity of the theory which underlies it, we can see that this is a poor argument. One might argue similarly that the individual's concern for social utility arises out of self-interest; i.e., we come to accept social well-being as a value because, by familiar processes of moral training, it is made to our self-interest to do so. Should we conclude then that it is irrational to be concerned about social utility except insofar as that concern serves our own well-being? Evidently, the proposed argument *for* consequentialism, to the extent that the consequences in question are social in nature, can as well be used *against* it. (And any other form of consequentialism will have extremely limited acceptance.) The argument, in short, involves the genetic fallacy, confusing considerations of how we come to accept a view with considerations of the view's justification. To be sure, a committed consequentialist may refer to the utilitarian origin of a controverted principle not in an effort to show it unjustified but rather to explain why his opponent accepts a principle which he deems unacceptable (as claiming moral authority in opposition to consequentialist considerations). Such a procedure is not fallacious, and may be used by one who is not a consequentialist. Thus, e.g., the moral prohibition against the use of contraceptive devices might be explained on the grounds that it arose at a time when the increase of human population had great social utility, that it became fixed as a moral principle − reinforced by the backing of religious authority, as were many moral principles − and was maintained as such in the face of relevantly different circumstances. This historical hypothesis − if a correct explanation − would not itself show the principle to be unacceptable; it would simply account for its being accepted. If one has a plausible explanation of his accepting a principle other than that the principle is intrinsically reasonable, then one may have a reason for (re-)examining his acceptance of the principle. But, of course, this leaves entirely open the question of what the outcome of that examination will be. Moral beliefs, like any others, presumably have a natural history; recognition of this fact can hardly serve to invalidate them, although it may be helpful in undermining what I have elsewhere called the 'morality mystique'.[6]

To one not bedazzled by that mystique, it should come neither as a surprise nor a disappointment that to a large extent both the justification and the explanation of the practice of holding persons obligable involve utilitarian or consequentialist considerations: such a practice is useful (to an extent, of course, not subject to *a priori* determination) in helping to bring about patterns of behavior deemed socially desirable. If we view the practice of holding individuals obligable — together with its subsidiary practices of praising and blaming, rewarding and punishing — as a means to the social control of behavior, then a number of facts about the practice fall into place.

More importantly from the point of view of *justification*, whatever socially desirable consequences the practice has constitute an evaluative reason in favor of the practice, and, like any positive evaluative reason, create an initial presumption that that (action, practice, or whatever) which it supports is thereby justified. It seems that this presumption can be defeated in the present case in two different, but not unrelated, ways (in addition, of course, to demonstrating the falsity of the underlying factual assumptions, e.g., that holding individuals obligable does have the consequences attributed to that practice). The first way involves a conceptual objection to the application of the term 'obligable', the second, a moral or evaluative objection, based on the claim that non-consequential evaluative reasons outweigh considerations of the social utility of the practice. Although the two kinds of objection are closely interrelated, it does seem that we can distinguish the claim that it is *unintelligible* to hold certain individuals obligable, from the claim that it is *unfair* or *pointless* to do so.

In any event, we have noted that application of the concept of obligability is (conceptually) restricted to rational beings; i.e., to beings capable of responding to reasons presented in an abstract manner. One may suppose that the explanation of this restriction arises from the historical identification of morality (and moral responsibility) with the law (and legal responsibility) and the recognition that no purpose is served by holding any being responsible to whom or to which the law cannot be promulgated. Whatever the historical merits of this supposition, a similar point would be served by restricting the application of obligability to rational beings: the considerations which enter into practical judgments tend to be highly abstract, requiring expression in language. The social control of behavior exercised on pre- or subrational animals necessarily involves a very restricted range of behavior (consider the discriminations which the possession of language enables us to make), and, of course, is effected by means other than the abstract presentation of reasons. The fact that as rational beings we are capable of acting on (linguistically presented) reasons which may provide genuine motivational alternatives to the sensory stimuli affecting us at a given time, is crucial for the justification of the practice of holding persons obligable, in a manner which is compatible with determinism but at the same time is sensitive to the libertarian's concern for freedom of choice as an element of obligability.

Recurring to an earlier schema[7] let us use the notion of *ability* so broadly as to make it the case that an agent's being able to ϕ, together with his having the desire (suitable motivation) to ϕ, constitute sufficient conditions of his ϕing. (Thus, we think of opportunity, knowledge, etc., not as factors coordinate with ability but as factors whose absence would serve to explain inability.) Assuming that each of these factors, ability and desire, is itself explicable in terms of sufficient conditions, and so on, this schema may fairly be said to be — for present purposes — deterministic. Assuming ability and desire sufficient for action is, one may note, substantially equivalent to the soft determinist's hypothetical analysis of ability. But, of course, the assumption is not intended as an *analysis* of 'X is able to ϕ', nor is there any suggestion that hypothetical substitutability is a sufficient condition of obligability. Still the soft determinist's emphasis on hypothetical substitutability serves to stress the role of the agent's motives for acting in our judgments of his obligability in a given case. Emphasis on these motivational factors is to be explained and justified by its social utility: assuming a relatively fixed repertoire of abilities and dispositions, an agent's desire to perform a certain action can be directly affected by the presentation of reasons. The view, moreover, that inability to do otherwise is always an absolving condition is to be explained, in part, by an exaggerated view of the ineffectiveness of holding persons obligable for their inabilities, which involves a failure to look beyond the immediate effects of the practice of holding persons obligable. The indirect effects of the practice must also be taken into account.

Expectation of sanctions (rewards, punishments, praise, blame) is the most obvious motivational factor with respect to the performance or non-performance of a given action. Sanctions, of course, need not be externally imposed. Thus, one may avoid doing something because he expects to suffer from guilt feelings if he does it. Nor need motives for acting involve expectations of sanctions. A suitably trained person may, e.g., be disposed to avoid acting unjustly, and thus be motivated to avoid a certain course of action when he comes to believe it unjust. Perhaps one can say generally that motivating reasons are apparent features of an action in virtue of which the action's performance or non-performance seems (*pro tanto*) desirable. Now the pragmatic justification of the practice of holding persons obligable depends principally on the fact that our having the practice and its concomitant set of sanctions (ranging upwards from the mild praise or blame naturally involved in having a favorable or unfavorable evaluation of an action made to an agent by the agent himself or by others) serves to modify a proposed action's appearance of (un-)desirability in socially useful ways. It does so most obviously and directly by the imposition of external sanctions for certain kinds of behavior. But it does so indirectly and much more fundamentally by leading to the development within individuals of a motivational pattern, of a certain set of dispositions to act in particular ways. This pattern constitutes one's *character*, and some of the dispositions are *moral virtues*. From the standpoint of social practice a good character is desirable because it tends to lead to desirable actions. But to maintain the practical primacy of *actions* is by no means to downgrade the importance of *character* or of the *virtues*; the practical significance of these features can scarcely be exaggerated.

Now, as Aristotle, for one, noted long ago, not only do our dispositions determine our actions, but our actions are the basis of our dispositions. ("We become just by performing just acts" – provided, of course, that these acts do not elicit a painful response.) The first point, that dispositions determine actions, suggested to Aristotle the first of two related difficulties for agent-responsibility which have troubled philosophers ever since. Essentially, the difficulty is this: how can we blame an unjust person for performing an unjust action (or praise a just person for a just one, etc.), since given the person's character, he could not have acted other than in the manner in which he did act? Aristotle's answer is that since we are responsible for our individual actions and that – unless we are excessively stupid – we know that performing unjust acts will lead to our becoming unjust, we are responsible for this aspect of our character. (Just as a man who has a physical disability as a result of his own actions is responsible for the disability, even though it is now beyond his power to affect.) Aristotle's answer is unpersuasive, especially if we suppose that insofar as a person's character is 'set', it is set in early childhood. In any event, prior to the time that an aspect of one's character is set (so that he is thenceforth 'programmed' to perform none but, say, unjust acts) he will have a tendency (albeit one not *determinative* of action) based on responses to previous actions, and so on, back to infancy. If an individual is unfortunate enough to have his untoward behavior go unreprimanded or otherwise unpunished, he will have an increasing and ultimately overwhelming tendency (beginning, again, in early childhood) to perform actions of this, say, unjust sort. This is just the kind of picture which some hard determinists draw.[8]

Perhaps there is somewhere an individual with a tendency to perform unjust acts which is so strong that it can only be called compulsive. But your normal unjust person hardly fits this characterization – or caricature: he is simply a person with an above average tendency to commit unjust acts. Even in the case of the most unjust of individuals it is totally implausible to suppose that his unjust tendencies cannot ever be overridden by other motives or reasons. In general, in disanalogy to the case of disability, a disposition or other motive to act can be overridden by the presentation of reasons at the time of a contemplated action. In this sense, motives may be said to incline without necessitating; i.e., *particular* motives (until operative) are capable of being outweighed – by other motives. This fact is of practical importance – but seems quite compatible with determinism. I shall return to it below.

Leaving aside the fantastic case of the Compulsive Unjust Man, we may recognize the similarities between the development of dispositions and of (dis-)abilities. Both develop, as Aristotle notes, as a result of our acting or failing to act in certain ways. This fact points to several ways in which there may be pragmatic point in holding persons obligable for actions or failures to act resulting from their dispositions or disabilities. The first is (the Aristotelian point) that knowing that one will be held obligable for actions tending to follow from one's dispositions or for failures to act certain to follow from one's inabilities or disabilities will provide a motive for performing actions leading to the desired abilities or dispositions.[9] The second is a very important related consideration, namely, that knowing that agents will be held obligable for actions flowing from their character will provide those entrusted with the rearing of the agents a strong incentive to provide their charges with education providing suitable abilities and dispositions. This incentive arises in part from concern for the well-being of the community, of which the moral teacher and the student are both members, and in part (especially where the teacher is also a parent of the future moral agent) out of strong concern for the reputation and well-being of the student. Note that despite this motivation, punishment of an individual for actions resulting (in part!) from failures in his moral training is not proxy-punishment, since the *punishment* is directed to the person who has performed the untoward act.

When one exercises one's imagination just a little, he quickly realizes the potential range of the indirect effects of a practice of holding persons obligable. Suppose, for example, that we held individuals morally responsible for being ugly. Thus, apart from the 'natural' disadvantages which ugly persons suffer, they might be thought justifiably to deserve to be punished for their 'crime'. The threat of this sanction might conceivably serve as a disincentive for ugly persons to produce offspring, thereby effecting the socially desired end of upgrading the level of beauty in the general population. Of course, the motivation might not be effective, but even if it were, we should surely find this extension of our practice of holding persons obligable unjustifiable — if not incoherent. I mention this case only to remind the reader that there may be a kind of pragmatic point to even a far-fetched practice of holding persons responsible, and, once again, that such a pragmatic advantage must be weighed against opposing considerations.

The final point that I wish to consider arises from Aristotle's concern that if individuals are moved to act by what appears good to them, and if they are not responsible for this appearance, then they cannot be responsible for their actions.[10] Aristotle's answer to this problem seems to be essentially that what appears as desirable or as an end to a person is a function of his character, and this, in turn, is the effect of earlier actions of the agent, for which he is responsible. But, of course, such a response merely transfers the question of the agent's responsibility for his actions to one concerning the earlier (character-forming) actions. Aristotle's view that persons act on the apparent good is essentially the same as the view that persons act on their strongest desires. (This may be thought of as clarification, not of Aristotle, but of the 'strongest desire' view.) The view leads to perplexity when conjoined with the OES-like supposition (or OES corollary) that to be responsible for an action one must be responsible for its sufficient conditions. If we can fully explain an action in terms of the agent's desires and abilities, it is still *his* action (he is [causally] responsible for it) so long as the desires and abilities are his. Or, if such 'explanations' are *too* good, the same point holds if desire and ability are thought of as (logically) sufficient conditions of action. Finally, if – perhaps as a matter of linguistic legislation – one holds that an agent *can* be responsible for his action only if he is responsible for its sufficient conditions, then not only do we have an unusual sense of 'responsibility', but in this sense moral responsibility can exist in the absence of (causal) responsibility (and we have all the more reason to put up with the unaesthetic 'obligability').

A large part of the justification of the practice of holding persons obligable for their actions on the assumption that an agent's desires (perception of the desirability of actions) and abilities are sufficient conditions for these actions, lies in the demonstration that the existence of the practice leads to modification of these desires and abilities in socially useful ways. I have given sufficient indication of how such modification is possible. Nor is there anything paradoxical in society's members instituting and preserving such a practice: they do so to the best of their abilities because of *their desires* for the social benefits which arise from the practice — or, rather, they *may* do so when the justifiability of the practice is challenged.

— "But that's just a pragmatic justification — on the deterministic assumption, it's unjust to hold persons obligable for their actions, because no one could ever have done other than he did." Having come full circle, we must surely be near the end (and my answer to the objection should be predictable). First, even if we grant the objector's point that holding persons obligable is (in perhaps some absolute sense) unjust, it does not follow that the practice of doing so is not (really) justified. To suppose that it does is to fall victim to the morality mystique. Second, in the absence of a clear and coherent indeterminist account in terms of which it is (absolutely) just to hold persons obligable for their actions, it is difficult to give much weight to the claim that it is unjust to do so on the determinist account.

Even though desires work quite differently from gears and levers, still the metaphorical talk of the 'push' or 'pull' of desires may yield an extremely misleading picture to one contemplating a deterministic account of human actions. It is for this reason that it may be useful to assimilate an account of actions in terms of desires to one based on the 'apparent good'. To be sure, if the appearance of overall desirability is sufficient to move a person to action, then the theoretical considerations are unchanged, but the *picture* is altered. This is so, I suspect, because one imagines the agent actively evaluating factors in coming to judgments of the relative desirability of different courses of action, rather than being pushed or pulled by desires with respect to them. Here we may note three points. First, the evaluative acts which culminate in a judgment of desirability are not themselves unmotivated. Second, the conflicting considerations which lead us to see the alternative actions as desirable may be just as well seen as pushes or pulls as may desires. Third, actions resulting from the (relatively small number of) cases of desires resulting from such conscious evaluative procedures (a) are still actions resulting from desires, and (b) are by no means coextensive with actions which are obligable.

We may note, finally, that on the account under consideration, although a desire to act constitutes, at the time of action, a sufficient condition for the action (assuming the agent's ability), still the consideration of reason by the agent up until that time may serve to alter the agent's desires with respect to the performance of the action. (Thus, e.g., an agent, about to perform a certain action, may refrain from doing so when he comes to realize some previously unforeseen consequences of the action.) We may note here a fundamental asymmetry between the ability and the desire to perform a particular action (though not between abilities and general tendencies to act — say, justly or considerately), namely that the desire for the particular action is subject to quick reversal. This fact is of practical significance. It tends to lead to the viewing of abilities as a fixed factor in the making of practical judgments, and of inabilities, hence, as not up to the agent and, indeed, as absolving conditions. It also leads to the claim that since any particular desire (expect, of course, under such a description as that of 'strongest desire', or 'operative desire') is defeasible, our actions are free. But the sort of freedom involved in this claim is one which is not incompatible with the assumption of determinism.

I have said little in this essay about freedom — and nothing at all about creativity or about the predictability of human actions. These omissions are deliberate. I have been concerned only with the question of the *compatibility* of determinism and obligability. For one whose concern is the defense of determinism, these other matters may be of fundamental importance. But for one whose concern is the compatibility question, they constitute only red herrings.

CHAPTER X

"WITH GOD ALL IS PERMITTED"

"By the command of God, death can be inflicted on any man, guilty or innocent, without any injustice whatever."

— Aquinas, *Treatise on Law*

"Without God All is Permitted."

— Dostoevsky, *The Brothers Karamozov*

In this final chapter, I shall discuss the view that morality must be or may be based on divine command or divine approval, the view, i.e., that what one ought (not) to do depends solely on what God wills. I shall discuss this view in part because of its historical practical importance, but principally because it represents a kind of position in terms of which there is but a single right-making consideration. I have already made clear my skepticism about the tenability of any such single-principle views. Part of my argument is designed to show the unacceptability of any view which holds that 'oughtness' is defined in terms of or otherwise constituted by the subjective reaction (e.g., approval) of any observer, divine or human, actual or ideal.

In the second part of the chapter, I want to pursue the question of the relationship of God and morality a step further, raising what may be called the New Problem of Evil. The Old Problem is that of reconciling belief in the existence of a morally perfect all-powerful being with the recognition of the existence of not inconsiderable natural and moral evil in God's creation. The New Problem is this: if we assume the Old Problem capable of resolution, the compatibility of the existence of God and of a meaningful system of morality comes into question. Briefly, then, in the first part of this chapter I shall question the view that morality is *based on* God's existence; in the second part, the view that the two are even compatible.

I.

Presumably, everyone has heard the oft-asserted claim of popular theology that without God — or at least, perhaps, without belief in God — morality is impossible. This familiar claim may be taken in at least two ways: that God is necessary to provide a *motivation* for acting morally, or that God is necessary to provide a *content* for morality. I shall be primarily concerned with the latter interpretation, particularly because of its relevance for two fundamental questions of ethical theory: Is there a single identifiable factor in virtue of which right actions are right? and Is the rightness of actions *constituted* by the subjective responses of some agent or agents? I suppose that the answer to both these questions is *No*, but if Divine approval is what makes right acts right, then the answer to both questions is *Yes*. Let us consider the matter.

First, however, let us briefly consider the view that the dependency of morality on (belief in) God is a matter of human motivation. The view is that only a belief in God, along, presumably, with the rewards and punishments that he will bestow on us, is sufficient to lead us to do what we ought. One may surely recognize that certainty of punishment — and indeed of just punishment and just reward — could hardly be better assured than by an arrangement in which sanctions are imposed by an omniscient, almighty, and morally perfect judge. But this fact, while helping to explain the conception of God held by those who presuppose a close tie between morality and religion — as well of course, as by those who require a suitable object of commitment or of worship — is simply irrelevant to the theory of practical motivation under considertion. And that theory seems simply false. For one thing, it rests upon (and incidentally encourages) the belief that persons can be motivated only by considerations of a narrowly selfish sort. Waiving the Kantian point that on this theory genuine *morality* would be impossible, since actions done solely out of hope of reward or fear of punishment are necessarily lacking in moral worth, we may note simply that persons are frequently motivated, e.g., by concern for the well-being, or, as the case of revenge shows, the ill-being, of others. For another thing, even if human motivation were always as self-centered as the view under consideration seems to presuppose, there is no empirical evidence for the supposition that only divine — as opposed, say, to social — sanctions can be efficacious. But this is more than enough discussion of a relatively unimportant point. In any event, if my overall argument is correct, and God and a serious morality are incompatible, then we need not seriously worry about whether belief in God as involving the expectation of divine sanctions or, say, simply our love of God must motivate us to be moral.

The more important interpretation of the claim that morality depends on God involves an un-Socratic reply to Socrates' familiar question in the *Euthyphro*, a question on which Wittgenstein at one time disagreed not only with Socrates but even with Schlick! Wittgenstein is quoted as having said the following to Friedrich Waismann in December, 1930:

Schlick says that in theological ethics there are two interpretations of the Essence of Good. On the shallow interpretation, the Good is good, in virtue of the fact that God wills it: on the deeper interpretation, God wills the good, because it *is* good. On my view, the first interpretation is the deeper: that is good which God commands. For this blocks off the road to any kind of explanation, 'Why it is good'; while the second interpretation is the shallow, rationalistic one, in that it behaves 'as though' that which is good could be given some further foundation.[1]

To be sure, Wittgenstein made this remark at a time when his metaphysical-linguistic views led him to relegate questions of value to the realm of the 'unsayable', where they are beyond — not beneath — the possibility of rational assessment. It would appear at least consistent with his later views, in which conventions, practices or forms of life serve as — or rather, in lieu of — foundations of knowledge, to allow that certain considerations may serve — within a given form of life — as *reasons* for particular moral claims. My present concern is not with such considerations, but with the answer Wittgenstein gave to the old Socratic question. I want to argue that any view on which attitudes, commands, etc. are said to be definitive or otherwise constitutive of moral concepts, is faced with conceptual difficulty. A divine command theory, moreover, is faced with peculiar difficulties of its own. Hence, If I am right, a little probing will show this theory appears *deep* only because it is muddy.

The *peculiar* difficulties of a divine command theory are connected with God's omnipotence. It is by no means clear that the notion of *willing* or *wanting* can have application in the case of an almighty being; in any case, it would be self-contradictory for such a being to desire or to will something to happen, and for it not to happen. Thus, unless we are prepared to identify what ought to occur or ought to be done with that which necessarily occurs or is done, thereby totally destroying the normal *point* of making practical judgments, we can hardly take God's *will* as the basis of moral value. Taking God's *favor* or *approval* as constitutive of moral goodness may or may not raise quite the same problem, but if it does not, it surely raises a rather stunning problem of Divine *Akrasia* . This problem, however it is described, is a central aspect of the Problem of Evil, and is much more resistant to solution than is the problem of human weakness of will. Whether or not we can speak intelligibly of a definite proattitude on the part of an omnipotent being which is not necessarily effected — and it strikes me that we cannot — it is surely not such a watered-down attitude which is embodied in a divine command or in any other supposed manifestation of God's conative state. If God were to command someone to do something, there would be no room for that person to question whether God really wanted him to initiate the action. Or, if — *per impossibile* — the person somehow knew that God did not *want* him to do what God had commanded, knew, i.e., that God had not uttered a *sincere* command, then it seems clear that God's sincere desire should take precedence over his insincere speech act. But if this is so, then the fundamental notion in any case involving a divine command is God's will; the former is significant only as a manifestation of the latter. (To be sure, God might will that a certain action take place as a result of his commanding it, and to that extent the command would not be *completely* otiose.) Now if God wills the existence of any states of affairs, including, of course, human actions, these states of affairs come into being. This follows necessarily from God's omnipotence. To pray that God's will be done is either to pray (to whom?) that God exist, or else to pray that a necessary truth be true. Nor will an appeal to 'free will' help here: if what God wills is that we perform certain acts *freely*, then (if it makes sense to say so) we perform them freely; i.e., we perform them. Thus it appears that God's omnipotence stands in the way of his will's (and *a fortiori* his commands') being the basis of our practical judgments.

Still, it is instructive to investigate a divine command or approval theory further, especially to illustrate certain further difficulties, some of which it shares with other theories which hold commands or attitudes to be *constitutive* of value. Let us, therefore, waive difficulties connected with divine omnipotence. Suppose now that we think of a divine command as a kind of Searlean speech-act: "I, God, hereby command you, Smith, to pay Jones five dollars", for example. Our theory would then have it that Smith ought, in virtue of that command, to pay Jones five dollars. Something of this sort seems to have been the intent of traditional divine command theories. As obvious difficulty confronting such a theory is that it seems logically possible that God should utter conflicting commands — he may have his own mysterious reasons for doing so — with the result that the performance of a particular action might become both right and wrong. This result would be especially embarrassing to those practitioners of theological ethics who suppose that basing morality on divine will obviates the deplorable 'relativism' of a humanly based ethical system.

Another difficulty is that provided by what is perhaps *the* standard objection to the view under consideration. This objection arises from what Wittgenstein appeared to take as a principle virtue of the view, namely its rendering moral choice irrational, or, perhaps, merely showing it to be so. This particular sort of irrationality has the result that *anything* might be morally good. Thus, suppose that someone, merely in order to relieve his boredom, kidnaps a small child, terrifies, tortures, and finally kills the child, dismembers its body, and mails it back, piece by piece, to its parents. Has the person in question done a morally admirable thing? Well, on the view under consideration, this would be a serious question, the answer to which would depend on whether or not God had commanded it to be done. " — But God, being good, would never command such a thing!" Clearly this common response is simply confused. It presupposes that God commands or forbids actions in virtue of their having certain characteristics which make them right or wrong, precisely the opposed logical order from that supposedly being defended. It reminds us, moreover, that it is very unclear what we mean, on this theory, when we say that *God* is morally good — are we praising God for his surpassing self-regard? Waiving this last point, a defender of the

divine command view *could* simply accept the suggested consequence of his view: God does not command us to torture or
murder, but if he did, these activities would be morally required.
And he might accuse his opponents of suffering from such physi-
ological defects as soft heads, weak stomachs, or bleeding hearts.
This is not wholly caricature: I take it that Abraham's initiating
steps to kill Isaac is not met with universal moral repugnance in
the theological community.

In addition to such difficulties, the theory under consideration
confronts seemingly insuperable epistemological difficulties in
the determination of what God approves or commands. After all,
God is not the sort of being who appears to most of us in the
normal course of events, and even if he were, there would be the
not inconsiderable difficulty of recognizing the appearance as an
appearance of *God*. On the view that God's command or approval
is alone constitutive of what is right, our epistemological difficulties multiply. First, there is the familiar point that we no
longer, on this view, have the possibility of appealing to ordinary
moral standards to help us determine which commands are likely
to have been issued by God. But, second, a point alluded to earlier
may be seen as raising epistemological difficulties. Suppose, for
the sake of argument, that we can identify divine speech-acts,
and that we have determined that God has done that which would
normally be taken as uttering the command that person P perform
action A. But suppose further that God, in fact, disapproved of
P's doing A. It would be very odd to maintain that when, as here,
divine approval conflicts with divine command, that the latter
should still be constitutive of genuine moral value. In giving the
command, God may wish to keep hidden his true attitude of
disapproval, meanwhile presumably approving of his own decep-
tion — again for his own mysterious reasons, or for none. We are
not entitled to say with Descartes and others that God is no
deceiver, thereby importing our own — external — moral standards

into the case; this is simply inconsistent with taking God's approval as constitutive of value. (I assume that a proponent of a theologically based ethic would have divine approval supersede divine command in case the two were in conflict.)

Let us turn to a fundamental difficulty which a divine command or divine approval theory shares with other theories which take subjective reactions to be definitive or constitutive of moral value. It may be stated summarily in the following dilemma: either the action – or other object of moral evaluation – is approved because of certain of its properties, or it is not. On the first alternative, it is these characteristics which are properly the basis for the evaluation (the criteria; the right-making or good-making properties); the approval is an inessential accompaniment, and surely is not constitutive of the moral value.[2]

But the second alternative – that the approval is not based on the characteristics of the action – not only would render the approval totally irrational, but seems itself not even to be coherent. The approval is irrational since a given action may be approved whether it is, e.g., a case of truth-telling or a case of lying. But this example shows why the alternative is incoherent – it presupposes that actions – and indeed merely contemplated actions, the objects of practical decision – can be identified (have an identity) apart from their characteristics, and this is absurd. Our dilemma, it appears, has only one genuine horn, and that one tells against approval theories of ethics, divine or otherwise.

But if it still appears that *God's* command could somehow make an action right, then there is one further level of paradox to which we may descend. (And, again, this difficulty applies not just to divine command theories, but to command and approval theories in general.) This level is reached when we see that the assumption that a command (by God, or by another being, real or ideal) is constitutive of an action's rightness reduces to absurdity. To see this, we need only to assume the possibility of second-order commands (or approvals) — a possibility not infrequently realized in everyday life (thus one in authority may command that an order of others' or of his own be disregarded; we may approve or disapprove of acts of approving on the parts of others — or ourselves, etc.), and to be clear about the relation of *being constitutive of*. To say, e.g., that *X*'s being *F* is constitutive of *X*'s being *G* (or that being *F* is what *makes* something *G*, or that something is *G in virtue of* being *F*) entails that there is no conceivable circumstance under which something could be *F* but not be *G*. Thus, for example, if a utilitarian claims that an action's maximizing utility is constitutive of its being right, then on this account any action which maximizes utility is *ipso facto* right, regardless of whatever features the action may have.[3] The view of utility-maximizing as constitutive of rightness has seemed subject to easy refutation on the basis of imagined counter-examples involving, e.g., execution of the innocent. Although I think that such objections to utilitarianism are ultimately valid, they are not *easy* to sustain, if only because it is open to the committed utilitarian (or perhaps one who, in his opponents' view, ought to be committed) to say that in any case in which the execution of the innocent would maximize utility it *would be* right.

Now, on a divine command theory, what God commands is left completely open, with the result that some particular action which we would normally account an atrocity — and one which did not even have great utility — might be commanded by God. On the theory it would be *ipso facto* morally required that the action be performed. This need not persuade a proponent of the theory that he is wrong: he need only deny that the case constitutes a counter-example to his theory. But if this dogmatism is taken as an act of faith, then in that faith there is no salvation.

This is so since we can conceive of a circumstance in which the claim that what God commands (or approves) is *ipso facto* that which we ought to do is falsified, namely that in which God commands us not to take his command (or approves our not taking his approval) as being constitutive of right action. Under this not inconceivable circumstance, if God's will were constitutive of what we ought to do, then it would not be; hence, it would not be. Thus, God's command or approval cannot be *constitutive* of an action's rightness. To help us see that the imagined circumstance is not totally implausible (although its mere implausibility would not be strictly relevant to my argument), we might speculate on reasons for God's commanding us not to take his commands as constitutive of right action. He might simply be concerned to preserve the autonomy of persons as moral agents. Or he might see that the epistemological difficulties in determining what he commands are so great as to make it more probable that persons would act in accordance with divine approval if they acted on standards other than that of divine command or approval. Or, most importantly, he might simply wish to help dispel the belief that divine will is constitutive of morality, since the belief is not only untenable, but has the implication that God's commands are completely arbitrary and capricious.

One doesn't find this divine command theory explicitly defended much nowadays. But it seems worth discussing because it sometimes seems to be a vague implicit assumption of those who maintain that religious belief is somehow essential to morality. From the point of view of moral theory, moreover, one who desires that there be a single factor which is constitutive of 'oughtness', must take some account of this ivew. And, finally, some of the fundamental considerations urged against this view are relevant to criticism of 'ideal observer' and other theories which hold attitudes to be definitive or otherwise constitutive of morality.

In any case, let this suffice as an argument against those who hold theistic belief or its object to be essential for morality, and turn to the stronger claim that God and morality actually stand in mutual opposition.

II

I have argued elsewhere[4] that on pain of moral skepticism we must recognize the irrationality of a belief in God; i.e., belief in an almighty, omniscient, and all-good Creator of this world. My argument turned on the traditional problem of evil, together with some considerations respecting the logic of our moral and other discourse. While some proponents of 'the argument from evil' claim that the existence of God is logically incompatible with the existence of evil, and hence, that the existence of evil demonstrates the non-existence of God, I maintained that this was too strong a claim. For one thing, of course, the theist might deny the existence of genuine evil — a point to which we shall return below. But, more importantly for most theists, who suppose that both God and evil exist, the argument for their incompatibility involves additional premises, at least one of which is open to question. These additional premises may be formulated as follows:

(1)   If there is a being who is omnipotent and omniscient, then that being can prevent the existence of evil.

(2)   If there is a being who is perfectly good, and who can prevent the existence of evil, then that being does prevent the existence of evil.

If we accept these two not implausible claims, then we cannot consistently accept the existence of a being who is all-powerful, all-knowing, and all-good (i.e., God) and the existence of evil. Of our two added premises, the first, which asserts that an omnipotent and omniscient being can prevent the existence of evil, may be accepted as straightforwardly analytic. To say that there is something which an omnipotent being cannot do, and which is such that its being done is neither self-contradictory nor inconsistent with its being done by the omnipotent being, is logically incoherent. It is the second of our added premises, however, which raises questions. It should be noted with respect to this premise that the claim that a perfectly good being would prevent evil if he could constitutes a moral judgment. It rests on the moral principle that it is wrong for a moral agent to permit evil when he can prevent it. Now I have maintained that moral generalizations are characterized by two not unrelated features: (1) they are not analytic, and (2) they are *prima facie* judgments, capable in given circumstances of defeat or qualification. These features are related, since insofar as a statement is subject to qualification or exception it is clearly not analytic. But the features are not to be identified: even a moral generalization incorporating a *'ceteris paribus'* clause designed to care for possible exceptions is not analytic. Thus, we need not suppose that one whose ethical principles differ from our own, even in a serious way, suffers from a *semantical* or *logical* confusion.

I should suppose that any logically forceful argument from the existence of evil to the non-existence of God must contain a moral judgment as a premise. If this is so, then the non-analytic character of such judgments suggests that the existence of evil is not *logically* incompatible with the existence of God. But this concession does not advance the theist's position a great deal: mere consistency is obviously only a minimally necessary condition for the rationality of a set of beliefs. The question of the truth value of the added premise remains. Granted that it is not *analytic* that it is wrong, even *ceteris paribus*, for a moral agent to permit evil when he can prevent it, is it true? If we take evil as represented by human (or animal) suffering, it seems obvious that the fact that an action is or involves the prevention of suffering constitutes a reason for its performance, and that the fact that an action involves a failure to prevent suffering constitutes a reason against its performance, and one which, in the latter sort of case, may require the specification of a reason (e.g., ignorance of suffering caused or permitted, prevention of greater suffering, or some other cost to the agent or to others) for its excuse or justification. The need for such a countervailing reason is the force of the *'ceteris paribus'* clause as it appears in moral, and other, generalizations − such a clause might be read as 'in the absence of sufficient reasons to the contrary'. Now it seems clear that it is wrong for a moral agent, *ceteris paribus*, to permit evil if he can prevent it.

This is still, however, insufficient to show that God would prevent suffering in the world: there is the *'ceteris paribus'* clause to be dealt with. There is, to be sure, a strong *prima facie* case for the view that God's omniscience and omnipotence render 'other things equal'. They obviously rule out the standard reasons which serve as excusing conditions for *our* failures to prevent suffering, e.g., ignorance, impotence, subjection to causal conditions, etc. Still God may have what Nelson Pike calls[5] 'morally sufficient conditions' for permitting his creatures to suffer. And, as Pike argues, we cannot prove, by showing that justifying reasons heretofore proposed by theistic apologists are unsatisfactory, that no morally sufficient reasons exist, simply because we can never be sure that we have exhausted all possible reasons.

But this fact is − or should be − of small comfort to the theist. For, unless we are prepared to grant that the mere *possibility* of there being morally sufficient conditions makes it rational − or not irrational − for us to suppose that an agent may be justified in permitting preventable suffering, even if we don't have the slightest clue as to what a plausible explanation of his behavior may be, then we must conclude that, in the absence of an adequate theodicy, belief in God is irrational in light of human and animal suffering. But if we do suppose that the mere possibility of an agent's having morally sufficient reasons for some *prima facie* wrong action or omission shows that it is rational to consider him justified in performing or failing to perform the action, then we are led to complete skepticism with regard to the practical evaluation of actions. For it is easy to imagine the *possibility* of excusing or of justifying conditions for any *prima facie* morally impermissible action. Thus, to escape the conclusion that an all-good God unjustifiably permits suffering, we must either adopt moral skepticism, or recognize the irrationality of belief in God, in the absence of an adequate and plausible explanation of why God permits suffering. And consideration of the sorts of justifying and excusing conditions that apply in the human realm makes it very unlikely that we shall find such an explanation. But the *possibility* that God has morally sufficient reasons for permitting suffering remains, and it will be instructive to examine the implications for morality if this possibility is realized.

I mentioned above the resolution of the problem of evil which involves denying that evil exists. This denial may be based on metaphysical claims to the effect that evil is *really* only the absence of goodness, or that reality and perfection are to be identified, or, at least, necessarily correlated. But whatever the basis of the view it should be obvious that its consequences for morality would be devastating. If there is no such thing as evil, then no matter what a person does, he can obviously do no evil. And if to do *evil* is to do that which is morally impermissible, then without the possibility of evil, the fundamental ethical distinction of the morally permissible and the morally impermissible has no possible application.

I want to suggest that any adequate theodicy will have the effect of denying the reality of evil, with the indicated devastating effects for morality. Consider first that prototypical theodicy which holds that this is the best of all possible worlds. This claim raises the following obvious difficulty for morality: whether I love my neighbor, or slay him, whether I drop rice to or napalm on a starving peasant, whether I take a child to a circus or into a gas chamber, in one respect, it makes no difference. No matter what I do, this remains, with God in his heaven, the best of all possible worlds. Now it may be claimed that the expression 'the best of all possible worlds' has no possible application.[6] So be it. Refraining from such talk will not eliminate our difficulty. For it there is an adequate theodicy — whether or not we can imagine what it might be like — then God has morally sufficient reasons for permitting (and ultimately, it would appear, for causing) everything that happens in his creation. But if God has such reasons, then there *are* such reasons, and any action or other event for which there are morally sufficient reasons is *ipso facto justified*, and involves — at worst — a merely *prima facie* evil. *How* it may be justified we do not know — God works in wondrous ways — but, if we are theists, we may have faith that it is.

Thus, if there are occurrences which are overall morally unjustified, then the (old) argument from evil succeeds, and there is no almighty, perfectly good being. But if there are no such occurrences, if God exists and has (and, hence, there are) morally sufficient reasons for everything that happens, then there can be no serious moral issues: every action, every policy, every state of affairs will be morally justified. If God has morally sufficient reasons for permitting any given state of affairs then that state of affairs is — overall — morally permissible.

One great merit of this abstract mode of argument is that it permits us to bypass the need to evaluate particular theodicies. The current favorite, the Free Will Defense, insofar as its central concept is clear, strikes me as utterly inadequate as a theodicy, even when it is supplemented by what I call the Credibility Gap Defense. This latter view involves the discounting of all the seemingly overwhelming evidence against the existence of an all-loving God on the ground that if the evidence for God's existence were not of at best mediocre strength we could not *freely* accept or reject belief in God! But without going into the merits of the Free Will Defense, I may indicate how my argument permits us to by-pass that proposed theodicy — and others. I shall thereby, I hope, clarify my argument.

Consider, then, the suffering caused by a particular human action, say, a case of rape. Waive the point that much human suffering is *not* caused by human action, let alone by free human action, and waive the question of whether and in what sense an action such as that under consideration is truly *free*. Ignore, also, the infringement of the *victim's* freedom. God could have prevented the rape, but did not. Being morally perfect, God had morally sufficient reasons for this act of omission, as for all his acts. One might suggest that only God could know what such reasons might be. But the Free Will Defender supplies an answer — of sorts — namely, that preventing the rape would have violated the rapist's freedom of action! At least some such absurdity seems implicit in taking the Free Will Defense as relevant to this sort of case. To be sure, that Defense is usually put in abstract terms as involving God's having the choice of creating robot-like creatures who automatically do 'right' or free agents who (freely) do a good deal of wrong. Waive the question of whether these alternatives are exhaustive. When this *wrong* is specified, we find cases of actions involving preventable suffering. Insofar as the Free Will Defense succeeds in a particular case, it does so only if God's prevention of the action and the suffering it causes involves a morally impermissible violation of the wrong-doer's freedom. To avoid controversy over substantive moral issues, let us, for the sake of argument, allow this seemingly absurd claim. Then the rapist's action may be characterized both as an exercise of the rapist's freedom and as the infliction of suffering on another. But on the Free Will Defense, God's permitting the action must show that its positive value under the former description outweighs its negative value under the latter. It appears that if the Free Will Defense — or any other theodicy — works, it works too well: God's having morally sufficient reasons for permitting *prima facie* evil suffices to show that the *prima facie* evil is only that, and that *overall* there is no evil at all.

This argument permits us to circumvent the difficulty mentioned above, namely, that we cannot run through all possible theodicies. We do not even have to evaluate any particular proposed theodicy. We are thereby relieved of the necessity of giving moral advice to God, or of making moral judgments of him or his works. To be sure, if so judging God is said to be blasphemous, then this sort of blasphemy is of a sort indulged in by those who proclaim the goodness of God. Of more philosophical importance, however, is the point that the argument here propounded does not depend on the resolution of substantive moral disagreements, a process which many philosophers see as logically or as epistemologically suspect. Whatever standards of moral permissibility may be thought to obtain, with God all is permitted.

NOTES

CHAPTER I. INTRODUCTION

[1] Henceforth I shall write 'his' as short for 'his or her'; 'he', as short for 'he or she', etc. It might be argued that this has always been done as a matter of standard practice. Still, I think it worthwhile to adopt the practice as a matter of deliberate policy so as not to appear to slight the justified concerns of feminists. Writing 'his or her' instead of 'his' every time is simply awkward, and I know of no other satisfactory alternative. (For those who suggest the use of 'their', as in 'everyone does their own thing', I can only ask, "does they really?") Were I addressing a mass audience, I should say more on this point. But I assume that the select group of readers of this work will not have its commitment to feminism, or, more generally, to humanism, affected by the use of a pronoun.

[2] v. Chapter VIII.

CHAPTER II. PRACTICAL REASONING, ACTION, AND WEAKNESS OF WILL

[1] See *Nicomachean Ethics*, Book Six, Chapter 10, 1143a1-10.

[2] Like other authors, I use 'obligation' here for want of a better substantive form for 'ought': 'oughtness', e.g., would be an unattractive addition to the language. But this usage must not mislead us into assimilating 'X ought to do A' with 'X is under an obligation to do A'. While statements of the latter form frequently provide reasons for those of the former, there are obviously all sorts of things we *ought* to do which are not matters of obligation, and there are many cases in which, all things considered, we ought not to fulfill obligations.

[3] As they are by William Frankena in his important paper, 'Obligation and Motivation in Recent Moral Philosophy' in *Essays in Moral Philosophy*, ed. A. I. Melden, Seattle, 1958, p. 44. My debt to this paper will be obvious.

[4] I shall not dicuss here the further question of whether the agent's being motivated to do A is 'conceptually connected' with his doing A.

[5] Cf. Frankena, *op. cit.*, pp. 40f.

[6] See next chapter.

[7] In 'Moral Dilemmas', *Philosophical Review* **LXXI**, 1962, pp. 144f.

[8] Cf. footnote 1, Chapter I.

[9] Cf., e.g., Nowell-Smith, *Ethics* (Oxford, 1957), p. 234.

[10] Some such thought may be involved in Gilbert Harman's claim that it is odd to say that "Hitler ought morally not to have ordered the extermination of the Jews". *The Nature of Morality* (New York, 1977), p. 107.

[11] Cf. e.g. W. D. Ross, *The Right and the Good* (Oxford, 1930), p. 152.

[12] I have said more on this point in my paper 'Miss Anscombe's Complaint' *Journal of Value Inquiry* **X**, no. 1, pp. 35–52.

CHAPTER III. THE DILEMMA OF OBLIGABILITY

[1] Cf. e.g. Donald Davidson, 'Actions, Reasons and Causes', *The Journal of Philosophy* **LX**, 23, pp. 685–700, reprinted in Bernard Berofsky (ed.), *Free Will and Determinism* (New York, 1966), pp. 221–240.

[2] See his 'Determinism, Indeterminism, and Libertarianism' reprinted in Berofsky *op. cit.*, pp. 135–159.

[3] *Ibid.*, p. 138.

[4] *Ibid.*

[5] Cf. Gilbert Ryle, *The Concept of Mind* (London, 1949), p. 69.

[6] For the terminology of 'hard' and 'soft' determinism, see James, 'The Dilemma of Determinism'. Reprinted in *Essays in Pragmatism* (New York, 1974).

[7] Broad, *op. cit.*

[8] Philippa Foot, 'Free Will as Involving Determinism' in Berofsky *op. cit.*, p. 97.

[9] Cf. my 'Obligability and Determinism: a Half-Asked Question', *Journal of Social Philosophy* **III**, 3, Sept. 1, 1972, pp. 12–14.

[10] Cf. C. A. Campbell, 'Is "Free Will" a Pseudo-Problem?' in Berofsky *op. cit.*, pp. 117f.

[11] Cf. e.g. Broad *op. cit.* (Consider, also, the Uncertainty Principle: its non-epistemological interpretations, whether correct or not, do not seem obviously self-contradictory.)

[12] I have in mind William James *op. cit.* It should be pointed out that James means nothing by 'chance' but 'absence of cause' and is simply avoiding an opportunity to be other than contentious.

[13] *Op. cit.*, p. 159.

[14] *Op. cit.*, p. 148.

CHAPTER IV. WAS FREE WILL A PSEUDO-PROBLEM?

[1] Broad, *op. cit.*
[2] Apart from acts of omission — which obviously must be taken into account on any adequate theory of obligability — most noncompelled but clearly caused doings, e.g., the person's sailing through the window in the example above, do not count as *actions*. (Also there is some dispute as to whether desires are to be accounted causes.) Even so, it is possible to imagine cases of actions other than acts of omission which are not obligable *because* they are caused. See, e.g., my 'Responsibility and the Causation of Actions', *American Philosophical Quarterly* **6**, No. 3, July 1969, p. 194.
[3] *Loc. cit.*, p. 240.
[4] 'Responsibility and the Causation of Actions', *loc. cit.*, p. 196.
[5] For a number of other difficulties with the use of 'try', see, e.g. Chisholm, 'J. L. Austin's Philosophical Papers' in Berofsky *op. cit.*, pp. 343 ff.
[6] Cf. P. H. Nowell-Smith, 'Ifs and Cans' in Berofsky, *op. cit.*, p. 325.
[7] As suggested by Nowell-Smith, *op. cit.*, pp. 333f.
[8] Cf. Chisholm, *op. cit.*, p. 345.
[9] R. Taylor, 'Determinism and the Theory of Agency' in S. Hook (ed.) *Determinism and Freedom in the Age of Modern Science* (New York, 1961), p. 226.
[10] This point has been noted by, e.g., Campbell and Taylor in the works previously cited.
[11] Cf. Campbell, *op. cit.*, p. 114.
[12] *Ibid.*, p. 113.
[13] See, e.g., J. J. C. Smart, 'Free Will, Praise and Blame' in G. Dworkin (ed.), *Determinism, Free Will and Moral Responsibility* (Englewood Cliffs, N. J., 1970), pp. 196–214.
[14] Campbell, *op. cit.*, p. 131.
[15] *Op. cit.*, pp. 156 ff.
[16] See his 'Freedom and Action' in K. Lehrer (ed.) *Freedom and Determinism* (New York, 1966), pp. 11–44.
[17] See his 'Determinism and the Theory of Agency' in Hook *op. cit.*, pp. 224–230.
[18] 'minimum unit', because one can intelligibly speak of groups of individuals, e.g. corporations or nations, as being blameworthy or praiseworthy, or rightly subject to reward or punishment.
[19] Cf., e.g. Hart and Honoré, *Causation and the Law* (Oxford, 1962).
[20] *Op. cit.*, p. 157.
[21] 'Freedom and Action' *loc. cit.*, p. 21.
[22] *Op. cit.*, p. 12f.

CHAPTER V. THE FLY IN THE FLYPAPER

[1] *Philosophical Investigations* I, §309.

[2] The best general expression of the view here under consideration is still perhaps A. I. Melden's *Free Action* (London, 1961).

[3] See, e.g., D. Davidson's 'Actions, Reasons, and Causes' *op. cit.*, pp. 221–240.

[4] See, e.g., Melden, *Free Action, op. cit.*, pp. 53 and 105. The rest of this paragraph, as well as the four paragraphs following, repeats what I have said in 'Responsibility and the Causation of Actions' *loc. cit.* For other criticisms of the doctrine under discussion, see Davidson *op. cit.*

[5] But we noted above in Chapter II that while an agent will *tend* to view his motivating reasons as justifying, he will not invariably do so.

[6] Cf. J. Wisdom, 'Philosophical Perplexity' and 'Metaphysics and Verification', both reprinted in *Philosophy and Psychoanalysis* (Oxford, 1953).

[7] The following six paragraphs repeat what I have said in 'Responsibility and the Causation of Actions' *loc. cit.*, pp. 189f.

[8] See, e.g. Melden *op. cit.*, esp. Chapter 8.

[9] Foot, *loc. cit.*, p. 97.

[10] Cf. Wittgenstein, *Philosophical Investigations* II, p. 213e: "Seeing an aspect and imagining are subject to the will. There is such an order as 'Imagine *this*' and also 'Now see the figure like *this*'; but not 'Now see this leaf green'."

CHAPTER VI. OUGHTS AND CANS

[1] In *Philosophical Papers* (Oxford, 1961), pp. 153–180.

[2] Broad *op. cit.*, p. 136.

[3] 'Responsibility and Avoidability' in Hook (ed.) *op. cit.*

[4] *Op. cit.*, p. 153.

[5] D. Rynin, 'The Autonomy of Morals', *Mind* LXVI, No. 263 (July, 1957), pp. 308–317.

[6] 'Freedom as the Absence of an Excuse', *Ethics* LXXIV, No. 3 (April 1964), pp. 161–173.

[7] *Ibid.*, p. 171.

[8] " ... freedom (i.e. substitutability) *must* be the absence of an excuse, if 'ought' really does *entail* 'could'." *Ibid.* p. 172. And conversely!

[9] Cf. Larence L. Heintz, 'Excuses and "Ought" Implies "Can"', *Canadian Journal of Philosophy* 5, No. 3 (November 1975) pp. 449–462, esp. pp. 453–457. Heintz, incidentally, appears to hold that if 'X cannot do A' means that X's doing A is contrary to natural law, or not within X's power, then

X's inability implies X's non-obligability. If 'implies' has the force of 'entails' I disagree with this claim on grounds presented above. More importantly, inability is not automatically an excusing condition: there are forms of culpable inability, just as there are forms of culpable ignorance. Thus, e.g., an agent's inability at a given time may be due to earlier actions of his own of a negligent − or even of a deliberate sort.

CHAPTER VII. UNPRINCIPLED MORALITY

[1] In 'Determinism, Indeterminism, and Libertarianism' *loc. cit.*

[2] On this point, and on the general topic of ethical relativism see the useful discussion in Richard Brandt's *Ethical Theory* (Englewood Cliffs, N.J., 1959), pp. 271−293.

[3] Cf. Philippa Foot, 'Moral Arguments', *Mind* LXVII (1958) pp. 502−513. Incidentally, I leave the fact-value distinction at a purely intuitive level, partly because it is so fundamental that an attempt to formulate it is very unlikely to be enlightening, and partly because, as my discussion indicates, I do not think that there is a sharp line to be drawn. On this point, in addition to Foot's paper, see John Searle's 'How to Derive an Ought from an Is', *The Philosophical Review* 73 (1964) pp. 43−58. It will be clear that I do not think feasible the project suggested by Searle's title if the 'ought' in question is that of the 'all things considered' categorical judgment.

[4] This sort of example merits some discussion, since it *may* suggest that my use of 'ought' differs somewhat from the ordinary − not, incidentally, a heinous offense if pointed out to one's audience. It may be suggested that there is nothing 'odd' about saying that someone *ought* not to have done something even though he had an *excuse* for doing it. For the most part, this suggestion appears to rest on a failure to note that 'excuse' is often used to signify an extenuating circumstance rather than what I have called an absolving condition. (Such a failure is particularly likely to affect the particular example I have given, since its reader is likely to imagine that the agent referred to is a *tourist*, i.e. a member of a species whose *gaffes* are never fully excused.) If 'excuse' (or 'excusing condition') is used for 'absolving condition', then there *is* something 'odd' about the statement in question, since it is approximately equivalent to the claim that someone ought not to have performed an action even though he was completely lacking in responsibility for its performance. (This claim is not just 'odd' but self-contradictory if 'obligability' is substituted for 'responsibility'.) What may be suggested, however, is that 'ought' and 'ought not' apply only to the suitability or untowardness of the action and not to the responsibility of the agent for its

performance. If these two notions can be coherently separated and if this restriction is embodied in the (?) ordinary use of 'ought', then it *is* one to which my use of the term does not conform.

[5] Cf. John Rawls' *A Theory of Justice* (Cambridge, Mass., 1971), pp. 42 f.

[6] *Op. cit.*, p. 43.

[7] See Mill's *Utilitarianism*, end of Chapter II. I have placed 'reverted' in quotes, since I am by no means convinced (by J. O. Urmson *et al.*) that Mill was a rule utilitarian despite the passage on 'abstinences' in Chapter II (" . . . the action is of a class which, if practiced generally, would be generally injurious, and . . . this is the ground of the obligation to abstain from it"). Most passages in the essay are more consonant with the view that the general principles are merely rules of thumb which provide a short cut in evaluating the utility of a particular act.

[8] *Principles of Morals and Legislation*, Chapter II. The principle of asceticism is that which takes increase of pain and decrease of pleasure as the moral criterion. Bentham's *argument* for the claim is defective, since it can be duplicated for any proposed criterion.

[9] Cf. G. E. Moore, *Principia Ethica* (Cambridge, 1903), pp. 187ff.

[10] On this point see, as the by now *locus classicus*, John Rawls *op. cit.*

[11] In addition to Rawls, *op. cit.*, see also, e.g., N. Rescher, *Distributive Justice* (New York, 1966).

[12] A contemporary example of what I call extreme anti-consequentialism is provided by Elizabeth Anscombe in her important 'Modern Moral Philosophy', *Philosophy* **33** (1958), pp. 1–19. For some discussion see Jonathan Bennett, 'Whatever the Consequences', *Analysis* **26** (1966), pp. 83–102, and Robert J. Richman, 'Miss Anscombe's Complaint', *The Journal of Value Inquiry* **X**, 1976, pp. 35–52.

[13] It should be remarked that Miss Anscombe's anti-consequentialism is not based on such a fear, but rather on her giving to the prevention of injustice an absolute lexical priority over other considerations, including, especially, consequential ones. The asboluteness of this priority is mitigated to some extent by her allowing that consideration of consequences may, in certain cases, enter into the determination of whether or not injustice exists, but there are, on her account, kinds of actions, including judicial punishment of the innocent, and, apparently, adultery, e.g., which are absolutely unjust, and for which there is no mitigation because of consequences. Those who, like W. D. Ross, hold that in some (extreme) cases consideration of consequences may justify even judicial punishment of the innocent are called by Miss Anscombe consequentialists, although this term is more naturally reserved for those who – like various utilitarians – hold that *consequences* should always be the decisive consideration in the practical evaluation of actions. Obviously, Miss Anscombe's account is subject to the objections raised earlier against the notion of the lexical ordering of moral maxims.

[14] With express misgivings, I so characterized my view in 'Miss Anscombe's Complaint' *loc. cit.* Since so many indefensible epistemological and/or metaphysical views, e.g. those pertaining to the certainty or necessity of 'intuited' propositions, or to peculiar 'non-natural' objects of intuition, are associated with or taken as central to intuitionism, I have no wish to insist on the term.

[15] Cf., e.g., Searle *op. cit.* I mention this kind of case since it seems to me that Searle places an inordinate amount of weight on the notion of institutional fact in the supposed derivation. Both institutional and non-institutional facts provide reasons for practical judgments; neither kind provides a generally sufficient reason for them.

CHAPTER VIII. BEYOND INTUITIONISM – A STEP

[1] *A Theory of Justice*, p. 34.

[2] This much anthologized essay appeared in *Philosophy* **XXIV** (1949), pp. 347–357.

[3] *Insight and Illusion* (Oxford, 1972), p. 152.

[4] See my review of Hacker's book in *The Philosophical Review* **LXXXIV** (1975), pp. 113–117.

[5] *Empiricism and Ethics* (Cambridge, 1967), p. 127.

[6] *Mind* **XXI** (1912), pp. 487–499.

[7] I am not suggesting that Prichard thought of himself as setting forth such an arbitrary stipulation; he clearly thought that he had arguments sufficient to show the impossibility of providing adequate reasons to support moral judgments. I am not here concerned to criticize Prichard's arguments. The interested reader might, however, consider the question of whether or not Prichard put too great a demand on something's being an adequate moral reason by requiring, in effect, that it be at one and the same time an adequate evaluative reason and an adequate motivational reason.

[8] Is the fact that a particular disagreement is not subject to rational resolution a sufficient ground for 'relativism' with respect to the subject at issue? The debate over whether it is, does not appear subject to rational resolution. If 'relativism' is the view that neither party to a dispute which is not rationally resolvable has a justified claim to truth with respect to the matter at issue, then this argument for relativism is self-defeating.

[9] See R. Firth's 'Ethical Absolutism and the Ideal Observer', *Philosophy and Phenomenological Research* **XII**, March 1952, pp. 317–345. I shall say more about the difficulties of an ideal observer theory when I discuss the divine command theory in Chapter X. For now, suffice it to say that such a theory takes the ideal observer's favorable or unfavorable reaction as definitive of

moral qualities. But since presumably such an observer's reactions would be based on features of the object or action judged, it would seem more reasonable to take those features as definitive of (or as providing criteria for) the moral qualities in question.

CHAPTER IX. "TO FORGIVE ALL ..."

[1] On this point, see in addition to Broad *op. cit.*, Wallace Matson's 'The Irrelevance of Free-will to Moral Responsibility', *Mind* **65**, 1956, pp. 489–497.

[2] One is reminded of Carlyle's familiar retort to Margaret Fuller's 'acceptance' of the universe.

[3] By 'reasons' here I mean those factors, especially the agent's desires and related beliefs, in terms of which we explain the action: the reference, then, is to what I called above 'motivating reasons'.

[4] The formulation may in a misleading – or, at least, in a question-begging – manner suggest that hypothetical substitutability is a sufficient condition of something's being an action: we normally wouldn't say "he would have acted otherwise if ... " unless we wished to suggest that he had *acted*. Generally, this suggestion is one which we do intend; in the rare cases in which it is not, we can perhaps, e.g., substitute 'behaved' for 'acted', where 'behave' is taken as a generic term which may, but need not, denote human actions.

[5] See Antony Flew's *The Presumption of Atheism* (London, 1976), pp. 98f. for a suggestion along these lines.

[6] See 'Miss Anscombe's Complaint', *loc. cit.* One aspect of the *mystique* is the supposition that moral belief has a totally different source from other sorts of belief.

[7] See Chapter V, above.

[8] Cf., e.g., John Hospers' 'What Means This Freedom?' in *Determinism and Freedom in the Age of Modern Science*, edited by Sidney Hoom (New York, 1961), pp. 126–142.

[9] This fact underlies the possibility of justifying 'strict liability'. See, e.g., Richard Wasserstrom's 'Strict Liability in the Criminal Law', reprinted in Herbert Morris (ed.), *Freedom and Responsibility* (Stanford, 1961), pp. 273–281. Strictly, 'strict' should be 'stricter', since there probably is no offense for which there is *no* excusing condition.

In any case, the notion of strictness – the lessening of the range of excusing conditions or the raising of the level of culpability for ignorance or inability – obviously carries over to our practice of holding persons obligable, and raises important question with respect to it. Making the practice stricter may have pragmatic advantages, but these must be weighed against obvious disadvantages. Some are themselves pragmatic, e.g. the time taken in the general teaching or learning of the desirable ability; others involve questions of social infringement on individual freedom or of lessened compassion. (This last point is especially relevant if the standards of culpability are set so high that it is difficult for many persons to meet them.)

[10] See *Nicomachean Ethics*, Book III, Chapter V, esp. 1114a 11.32ff. and 114b 11.14ff

CHAPTER X. "WITH GOD ALL IS PERMITTED"

[1] A. Janik and S. Toulmin, *Wittgenstein's Vienna* (New York, 1973), p. 194. Nothing in particular turns on the attribution of this view to *Wittgenstein*.

[2] Failure to recognize this point may be due to 'the craving for generality': a philosopher recognizes the difficulty, or the impossibility — which we have noted at length above — of specifying universally applicable conditions of an action's being right; and notes further that a person's (sincere) claim that an action is right is always accompanied by that person's approval of the action. The philosopher then concludes that this approval, the only common feature of acts adjudged right, is *ipso facto* all that does or can constitute the act's rightness. But, of course, the speaker's approval is a condition only of the sincere *assertion* or *judgment* that the action is right, and is not a condition and *a fortiori* is not constitutive of the action's *being* right. Cf. the analogous case of a speaker's belief that *p* as a condition of his sincerely asserting that *p* is true. Should we say that a speaker's (which?) belief is *constitutive* of truth?

[3] This view is to be contrasted with one which holds, e.g., that maximizing, or indeed increasing, utility, is a reason for performing an action, or is something we ought, *ceteris paribus*, to do, or is a *prima facie* obligation, etc. A divine command or approval theory is hardly open to such an interpretation.

[4] 'The Argument from Evil', *Religious Studies* **4**, No. 2 (April, 1969), pp. 203–211.

[5] In 'Hume on Evil' in *God and Evil* (Englewood Cliffs, NJ, 1964), p. 88.

[6] 'Alvin Plantinga, *inter alia*', makes this claim in *The Nature of Necessity* (Oxford, 1974), p. 168.

INDEX